The Fiction of Anne Tyler

THE FICTION OF
Anne Tyler

EDITED BY C. RALPH STEPHENS

UNIVERSITY PRESS OF MISSISSIPPI
Jackson and London

Copyright © 1990 by the University Press of Mississippi
All rights reserved
Manufactured in the United States of America

93   92   91   90   4   3   2   1

The paper in this book meets the guidelines for permanence and durability of the Committee on Production Guidelines for Book Longevity of the Council on Library Resources.

Library of Congress Cataloging-in-Publication Data

The fiction of Anne Tyler / edited by C. Ralph Stephens.
    p.   cm.
    Includes bibliographical references.
    ISBN 0-87805-435-9 : $27.50
    1. Tyler, Anne—Criticism and interpretation.   I. Stephens, C.
Ralph (Charles Ralph)
PS3570.Y45Z65   1990
813'.54—dc20   89-49306
                                                                   CIP

British Library Cataloguing-in-Publication data available

Contents

Acknowledgments

I am grateful to a number of people for help with this volume: to my wife Martha, for her patience, encouragement, and assistance at many turns; to all of the contributors, who were unfailingly responsive to my requests and punctual in meeting deadlines—especially to Anne Ricketson Zahlan and Virginia Shaefer Carroll, for useful suggestions for my introduction; to my colleagues at Essex Community College, who gave generously of their time and counsel; and to Ginny Miller, whose help with correspondence and proofreading made this job much easier. I owe a special debt of gratitude to Charles A. Fecher, friend and H. L. Mencken scholar, for invaluable editorial assistance and advice.

Grateful acknowledgment is also made to the following:

Alfred A. Knopf, Inc., for permission to quote from the eleven novels of Anne Tyler.

Atlantis: A Women's Studies Journal, for permission to reprint Mary J. Elkins' article, *"Dinner at the Homesick Restaurant:* Anne Tyler and the Faulkner Connection," originally published in *Atlantis,* 10 (Spring 1985), 93–105.

The University of California Press, for permission to reprint "Anne Tyler: The Tears (and Joys) Are in the Things," chapter 5 of Margaret Morganroth Gullette's *Safe at Last in the Middle Years: The Invention of the Midlife Progress Novel: Saul Bellow, Margaret Drabble, Anne Tyler, and John Updike* © 1988 The Regents of the University of California.

Introduction

Few contemporary American writers of fiction have been as steadily productive as Anne Tyler, and fewer still have garnered a devoted and sizeable popular audience *and* the solid respect of their peers. At midlife and one assumes midcareer, Tyler has achieved a record of publication that is little short of extraordinary: eleven novels, nearly four dozen short stories, and reams of articles and highly regarded book reviews.

Such distinguished fellow writers as Gail Godwin, Joyce Carol Oates, and Larry McMurtry have praised Tyler's work in perceptive reviews of it. John Updike has paid particular attention to Tyler, enthusiastically reviewing for *The New Yorker* each of her novels since *Searching for Caleb* (1976). Declaring her in that first review a writer "not merely good, [but] *wickedly good*,"[1] Updike has repeatedly extolled Tyler's "remarkable talent"[2]—noting her "power to see and guess and know"[3] and her ability to observe life "with a tolerance and precision unexcelled among contemporary writers,"[4] specifically evoking the names of John Cheever, Flannery O'Connor, Carson McCullers, and Eudora Welty.[5] Indeed, Welty has long counted herself among those who "love and admire" Tyler's work, as have Tyler's former writing teacher Reynolds Price and fellow novelist Doris Betts.

It has been a matter of curiosity to many discerning readers that Tyler has been slower to attract scholarly assessment. In his 1982 *New Yorker* review of her ninth novel, *Dinner at the Homesick Restaurant*, John Updike observed wryly that Tyler's "humane and populous domestic novels have attracted (if my antennae are tuned right) less approval in the literary ether than the sparer offerings of Ann Beattie and Joan Didion . . . ."[6] And Sarah English noted in a long piece on Tyler in the *Dictionary of Literary Biography Yearbook 1982*, "In spite of her now impressive body of work, [Tyler's] fiction has received little academic analysis. That absence of attention is puzzling, since Tyler is a serious, gifted, prolific writer whose fiction has been consistently admired by important critics and fellow novelists."[7] She concluded, "It is time for critics to stop worrying about the direction her work is taking and to look seriously at what she has accomplished."[8]

While this situation has recently begun to change,[9] it is still true that Tyler's fiction has not received the careful attention it deserves. To date, the greatest concentration of such attention to Anne Tyler occurred at a national symposium on her fiction sponsored by Essex Community College in Baltimore on April 21–22, 1989. Most of the essays in this volume have been selected from papers given at that symposium; they testify to the high regard Tyler enjoys among serious readers—and to the fertile territory for critical investigation her work offers. The writers of these essays advance one common argument: the present, however early it may turn out to be in Tyler's career, is not too soon for close and thoughtful appraisal of her achievement. Taken together, their discussions constitute something of a potpourri of varied tone and wide-ranging interest, with emphasis here on issues in individual novels, there on recurrent themes and topics in Tyler's canon—the interplay between life and art, the tensions between individual identity and the demands of family, the centrality of houses and neighborhoods.

The opening essay, Doris Betts' "Tyler's Marriage of Opposites" (a revised version of her symposium keynote address), focuses on Tyler's latest novel, *Breathing Lessons,* to identify and examine the dynamics of opposing tensions as a key structural principle in her novels. Several of the essays which follow examine Tyler's fiction through the lenses of interdisciplinary scholarship, expanding onto new ground discussion of topics addressed earlier by reviewers and critics: Virginia Carroll, for example, looks from a sociological perspective at the conflicting roles of kinship in five novels; Barbara Carson, Joseph Wagner, and Anne Zahlan invoke varieties of traditional and contemporary psychoanalytic theory to explore the central issues of individual novels—Rogers and Maslow for *Celestial Navigation,* Freud and his descendants for *Dinner at the Homesick Restaurant,* Freud and Lacan for *The Accidental Tourist.*

Other essayists argue the importance of specific elements in Tyler's fiction: Theresa Kanoza, the mentor role of Tyler's unconventional mothers-in-law; Frank Shelton, the function of residence in her fictional method and theme; Sue Inman, Tyler's artist figures as links to Tyler's own view of the artistic process. In his essay on *Morgan's Passing,* Gordon Taylor suggests ways in which Morgan Gower's refusal to be confined to a single identity and his compulsive reinvention of himself (his "self-artistry") have parallels not only in other Tyler characters but also in Tyler's own resistance to definition and classification.

Three writers in this collection are interested in Tyler's relationship to other writers: Margaret Gullette in Tyler's affinity with Bellow, Drabble, and Updike, whom she regards as creators of a new genre of "midlife progress novels"; Carol Manning and Mary Elkins in parallels between Tyler and Southern literary antecedents—Manning looks at a kinship Tyler has openly acknowledged, Elkins at one Tyler denies.

Finally, Susan Gilbert, in "Private Lives and Public Issues: Anne Tyler's

Prize-winning Novels," discusses Tyler's last two and most publicly cele-
brated novels, which raise questions for some readers about Tyler's relation
to public issues. Gilbert offers a view radically different from the one ten-
dered by Betts.

These essays constitute an important addition to the present limited body
of Tyler scholarship, and they begin to suggest directions for future critical
inquiry. The richness of Tyler's work and the need for continued scholarly
discussion are manifest in the many questions, issues, and themes that
remain to be addressed. For instance, Tyler's comic sensibility and the
important roles humor and irony play in her fiction have often been remarked upon by reviewers but have only begun to be investigated crit-
ically;[10] the sources of her humor and its thematic and structuring func-
tions in her work clearly merit fuller attention. In his review of *The
Accidental Tourist,* Updike observed that a reason some critics and readers
have had trouble taking Tyler completely seriously is that "we have lost
familiarity with the comedic spirit,"[11] a point worth broader application to
Tyler's fiction.

Tyler's detractors have objected to the avoidance in her fiction of social
problems and political issues, claiming that her skill is largely put to limited
if not irrelevant ends, that she is a writer who hovers above life, creating
charmingly eccentric characters whose struggles seem pointless, a writer
whose point of view wavers between bemused detachment and "life-affirma-
tion" which largely ignores its reality. Noting her Quaker heritage (which
includes several years of childhood in a North Carolina commune, a social-
worker mother and a father who has taken an active role on the Friends'
Service Committee) and her marriage to Iranian psychiatrist Taghi Modar-
ressi, other readers argue that Tyler has hardly been insulated from social
concern or world affairs, and that her alleged "passivity" belies a studied,
wise politics of a different sort than strident activism. Critics of a political
turn of mind, perhaps especially Marxists, are sure to want to argue such
interpretations.

As already noted, interdisciplinary scholarship—anthropology, psychology, structuralism—is reflected in several of the essays in this collection.
Other promising cross disciplinary approaches come to mind easily: feminism, new historicism, cultural approaches to Tyler's renderings of the "dislocations" of U.S. society from the sixties through the eighties, for example.

Closer analysis is needed of Tyler's craftsmanship: her use of language,
her style, her fictive strategies—especially of her narrative technique in the
light of contemporary or contemporarily popular theories of narrative.
Tyler's settings, particularly her Baltimore geography, warrant more detailed study—inviting also comparison with other writers who exploit or
invent their own territory. (Among contemporary microcosm-makers,
William Kennedy is a likely choice.)

Other themes and approaches that should attract scholars include the influence on Tyler's work of Quaker values, the antihero as a recurring figure in her novels, her dream imagery, the variations on the theme of feeding, the displaced sexuality in her characters and the marked sexual reticence in her fiction, Tyler's relation to other writers and traditions—to other women writers, to Southern writers, to realism, to American literature, and (particularly in the light of her graduate training) to Russian fiction—especially Chekhov.

Her short stories, though included in several anthologies, need to be collected, and her achievement in that genre assessed. Her book reviews and articles (and her introduction to *The Best American Short Stories 1983*)[12] shed light on her own critical theory, but they have not yet been carefully examined, nor has her own work been examined in the light of her published views on writing and writers.

The first aim of literary scholarship is always—or should be—increased insight and renewed pleasure in the work it examines. If readers of Anne Tyler are so moved by the essays in this collection and if additional inquiry into the operations of her fiction is stimulated by them, this volume will have served a useful end.

C. R. S.
Baltimore, 1989

NOTES

1. "Family Ways," 52 (29 March 1976), 112.
2. "Loosened Roots" [rev. of *Earthly Possessions*], *The New Yorker*, 53 (6 June 1977), 130.
3. "Family Ways," p. 112.
4. Ibid.
5. "Imagining Things" [rev. of *Morgan's Passing*], 56 (23 June 1980), 97.
6. "On Such a Beautiful Green Little Planet," 58 (5 April 1982), 195.
7. (Detroit: Gale Research, 1983), p. 187.
8. Ibid., p. 193.
9. Beginning in 1983, scattered critical articles have appeared in *The Southern Literary Journal, Southern Review, The New England Review and Bread Loaf Quarterly, The Hollins Critic, Atlantis, Mississippi Quarterly,* and *The Southern Quarterly,* the last containing an important assessment of Tyler's work by Doris Betts, reprinted in *Women Writers of the Contemporary South,* ed. Peggy Whitman Prenshaw (Jackson: University Press of Mississippi, 1984). *Contemporary American Women Writers: Narrative Strategies,* ed. Catherine Rainwater and William J. Scheick (Lexington: University Press of Kentucky, 1985), contained a substantive, ground breaking essay on the relationship between Tyler's concern with family relationships and her narrative techniques, "Anne Tyler: Medusa Points and Contact Points," by Mary F. Robertson, and "A Bibliography of Writings by Anne Tyler," compiled by Elaine Gardiner and Catherine Rainwater, a useful update of Stella

Nesanovich's "An Anne Tyler Checklist, 1959–1980" in *Bulletin of Bibliography,* 38 (2) (April–June, 1981), 53–64. Anne R. Zahlan contributed to *Fifty Southern Writers after 1900: A Bio-bibliographical Sourcebook* (Westport, CT: Greenwood Press, 1987) an extended scholarly overview of Tyler's career, including a detailed discussion of major themes in her first ten novels and a carefully researched survey of criticism. At least five doctoral dissertations on Tyler have been completed: Stella Nesanovich's "The Individual in the Family: A Critical Introduction to the Novels of Anne Tyler" (LSU, 1979), Dorothy Faye Sala Brock's "Anne Tyler's Treatment of Managing Women" (North Texas State University, Denton, 1985), Judi Gaitens' "The Web of Connection: A Study of the Family Patterns in the Fiction of Anne Tyler" (Kent State, 1988), Karen Linton's "The Temporal Horizon: A Study of the Theme of Time in Anne Tyler's Major Novels" (Uppsala University, Sweden, 1989), and Deborah Pope, "Character and Characterization in the Novels of Anne Tyler" (University of Mississippi, 1989); several others are in progress. Two book-length studies of Tyler's work are forthcoming: Joseph C. Voelker's *Art and the Accidental in Anne Tyler* (Literary Frontiers Series) (Columbia: The University of Missouri Press, 1989) and Alice Hall Petry's *Understanding Anne Tyler* (Greenville: University of South Carolina Press, 1990).

10. See Anne Zahlan's essay in this collection; see also Bradley R. Bowers, "Anne Tyler's Insiders," *Mississippi Quarterly,* 42 (1) (Winter 1988–89), 47–56.

11. "Leaving Home" [rev. of *The Accidental Tourist*], *The New Yorker,* 61 (28 October 1985), 111.

12. Ed. with Shannon Ravenel (Boston: Houghton-Mifflin, 1983), pp. xi–xx.

NOTES ON REFERENCES

Quotations from the novels of Anne Tyler are given in the body of the text with the following abbreviations:

AT	*The Accidental Tourist* (1985)
BL	*Breathing Lessons* (1988)
CN	*Celestial Navigation* (1974)
CW	*The Clock Winder* (1972)
DHR	*Dinner at the Homesick Restaurant* (1982)
EP	*Earthly Possessions* (1977)
MEC	*If Morning Ever Comes* (1964)
MP	*Morgan's Passing* (1980)
SC	*Searching for Caleb* (1976)
SDL	*A Slipping-Down Life* (1970)
TCT	*The Tin Can Tree* (1965)

All page references are to the original hardcover editions published by Alfred A. Knopf, Inc., New York.

The Fiction of Anne Tyler

Tyler's Marriage of Opposites

DORIS BETTS

A friend at Chapel Hill and a fellow Tyler fan, Professor George Lens-
ing, once remarked that as he moved along library shelves choosing
books, he would often open an unfamiliar novel and examine its first
and last sentences as clues to whether or not he would enjoy reading the
whole.

(Naturally a thrust of acid pierced me during instant recall of my own
unsatisfactory opening and closing sentences.)

However, once I had become about the millionth reader to notice that
Jane Austen's novels open by discussing money and progress toward concluding with marriage and security, I decided to examine Anne Tyler's early
novels and test how her fictions start and stop. If home is said to be the place
where you can scratch anything that itches, home is central to many Tyler
openings—and so is somebody's itch to get away from it.

"When Ben Joe Hawkes left home . . ." are the opening words of *If
Morning Ever Comes* (1964), for instance, but the reader soon learns that
Ben Joe is actually enroute home *again* to Sandhill, North Carolina, because
his sister has left *her* home and husband and recently fled back to *their*
parental home. *The Tin Can Tree* (1965) begins with the statement, "After
the funeral, James came straight home . . . ." That funeral is only one of
Tyler's many opening funerals initiating her plots, this one to bury Janie
Rose Pike, aged six, killed in a tractor accident. One of my two favorite Tyler
novels, *Celestial Navigation* (1974), opens with Amanda's only section of
narration, in which she introduces her brother Jeremy Pauling, a 38-year-
old bachelor who has never left home at all, and is now telephoning to
summon her back home because of their mother's death. A mother is also

1

dying on the first page of my second favorite Tyler novel, *Dinner at the Homesick Restaurant* (1982); and during the first scene of *The Accidental Tourist* (1985, Tyler's first novel to be made into a movie) because of another random, meaningless child's death—the murder of their son Ethan in a fast-food restaurant—the marriage of Macon and Sarah Leary is dying. The widowed Mrs. Emerson needs a "clock winder" (*CW*) after a death, her husband's. And in *Breathing Lessons* (1989), Maggie and Ira Moran will spend almost half the novel attending a funeral that echoes, even attempts to duplicate, the dead man's wedding.

This rather amusing funeral first appeared as a separate story in a holiday issue of *The New Yorker,* July 4, 1988, entitled "Rerun." In her eleventh novel, this funeral, Max Gill's sendoff to his *eternal* home, has the same cause-effect function of generating the story as do funerals for Pearl Tull or Mrs. Pauling, or even in Tyler's third novel, *A Slipping Down Life* (1970), precipitating change. Here the funeral comes near the end as Evie returns home from arranging last rites for her father, only to discover her husband Casey in bed with her best friend. As usual, death is not Tyler's final word—the novel concludes after Evie has left Casey to await alone the *birth* of their baby.

In Anne Tyler's reality, there is always life after death, literally, in the plots; the marriage of opposites produces it. In *Breathing Lessons* the two who respond to death with lively sex and are found in bed together after Gill's funeral are a couple twenty-eight years married, Ira and Maggie Moran.

Perhaps Tyler's steady and positive counteracting of death by love or new life, her italicized hope which some attribute to her Quaker background, are partial reasons five of Tyler's novels have been Book-of-the-Month Club selections, and *Breathing Lessons,* although a smaller work than my two favorites, received the 1989 Pulitzer Prize. Many Tyler novels begin where other contemporary writers would write "The End." Death only appears to conclude events, then it becomes her precipitating event for change, plot, and subplot. I can imagine *For Whom the Bell Tolls* would come out of Tyler's typewriter following Maria on her headlong horseback ride behind Pilar into a different life; or that Tyler's Chapter One might show Nick Carraway departing from final rites for Gatsby enroute to new adventures in the midwest. Although her plots do include other crises—quarreling, suicide, death, even sex, though rather understated sex—in Tyler's fiction climactic events become early cause; her characters work through them toward later denouement or conclusion. She remains more interested in how her people survive and persist *beyond* crisis during their long, steady, three-meal-a-day aftermaths.

Though her affirmations have won her a wide audience, her insistence on chronicling what the *Baltimore Sun* called "the mundane"[1] has had two

2

interesting effects on her literary career. Her popularity makes some literary critics wary that her vision may be too rose-colored. Yet, despite her popularity, she has never become lively copy for *People Magazine* because her own life has included one long marriage and motherhood, nor does she get interviewed about the pleasures of domesticity for housewives' magazines. The reclusive Ms. Tyler would never let Barbara Walters inside her front door. Though she did attend the premiere showing of *The Accidental Tourist* where she was seated in a theater section roped off from others, she has since her first novel appeared in 1964 secluded herself to write, and maintained equal unconcern about being popular, fashionable, or avant garde.

Make your own list of newsworthy literary categories that, like Procrustean beds, will not contain her comfortably. Does Tyler write the self-consuming metafiction of Coover, Barth, Barthelme? Would you classify Anne Tyler as a post modernist? How about mixing genres—does she blend history with fiction like Doctorow, journalism with fiction like Capote and Mailer? Does she write Writing with a capital-W like Updike; is she a Raymond Carver minimalist? A conscious practitioner of artifice like John Fowles? Is she locked into her despairing existentialist self? Have you heard Anne Tyler deconstructed often? Would she agree with Walker Percy that it is "better to be a drowning man than alive and well in East Orange?" Since she grew up in North Carolina, does she fit the profile for the self-conscious "Southern" writer? Which Tyler novel can be categorized as surreal, topical, political? Does she belong to the '80's "brat pack" in whose brightly-lighted, big-city prose we always hear the fast click-click of computer keyboards? Is she a Maryland version of those women writers producing mall and K-Mart fiction? Why isn't Anne Tyler as flashy as beatniks, yippies, yuppies? Would Geraldo Rivera cross the street to ask her about pornography?

Can we even call Anne Tyler by that capital-F word, *Feminist?* One conclusion I draw from *Breathing Lessons* is that Tyler understands the differences between the male and female consciousness more intimately than Gloria Steinhem; but because Tyler's women often collaborate with the chauvinist enemy, and by staying married try to merge those opposites into one flesh, her heroines are seldom angry enough to star in the average Women's Studies syllabus. Passion or rage do not deter Anne Tyler long. On their wedding night, when Maggie Moran comes out wearing her sheer white nightgown and Ira sucks in his breath in awe and admiration, Maggie "thought that would go on forever." Tyler writes about all the rest of married life that goes on instead.

Since 1964, unencumbered by literary trends and categories, Anne Tyler has kept moving along her own main line, employing a vision that may seem rosy to contemporaries because it is more classic than romantic. Her eleven novels reverse today's more typical alienated linear progression by moving her plots from grave to cradle, from death to birth or rebirth, with themes which only sink briefly, then rise from the depths onto ordinary weekday plateaus where she presents, as she has said, "how people last." Her characters oppose, juxtapose, and resolve; and they perform this complex dance of life inside the family, although during her publishing career demographics have indicated a decline in or at least reshaping of the nuclear American family. While some would say the family has almost died out during the last quarter century, Tyler's families break, mend, and persist; she seems in tune with the Moroccan proverb: "None but a mule denies his family." However modified, this family unit remains on center stage where her characters play out, as she told Mary Ellen Brooks, "how people manage to endure together—how they grate against each other, adjust, intrude and protect themselves from intrusions, give up, and start all over again in the morning."[2] You can't get much closer to true Women's Studies than that nor, indeed, to the mood of the final page of *Breathing Lessons*. When Cecil B. deMille was asked why he made so many films based on the Bible, he shrugged: "Why let 2000 years of publicity go to waste?" Tyler is unwilling to waste the ancient human microcosm arranged around the hearth, and especially the family unit of the last several centuries.

Had Friedrich Hegel been a wife and mother forced to do his thinking between the crib and washing machine, Hegelian philosophy might have sung the music-of-the-spheres to Anne Tyler's tune: Thesis/Antithesis/Synthesis—all of them banging together in a domestic blend down the hall, or being stirred into wistful synthesis at the dinner table, or sometimes resplit by slamming screen doors. Novelists typically arrange their selected polar opposite characters and contrasting themes into struggles between protagonists and antagonists, but Tyler's protagonists also take—or long to take—that third reconciling step in the direction of synthesis. She almost seems as homesick as Ezra Tull to feast on a happy ending.

Yet Tyler usually resists the temptation to attach with Velcro a hackwriter's happy ending to her final page. She tries to make her characters earn solutions, step by step, or be dragged into happiness as Macon Leary is, by a dog and a dog trainer. Having learned in her own kitchen the art of dividing a cake so everybody thinks he got the biggest slice, sometimes Tyler does try—like Maggie Moran—to work more magic for her surrounding characters than they can digest and she may, in *Breathing Lessons*, dramatize her own artist-conflicts through Maggie. But usually, if Jane Austen's novels begin with money and end with marriage, Anne Tyler's stop short of absolutely happy endings to close with small convergences: people make temporary rest stops on life's journey; they take catnaps in the marriage bed or drop anchor at sandbars somewhere in the relentless flow of time. Even when Tyler's last sentence seems to make a temporary truce with fate, readers suspect that if they could read onward beyond her back cover, her still-fated people would soon be setting off again.

4

The contrasts Tyler sets up within families are part of the general pattern of contrasts in fiction. The fantasy world of Don Quixote needs the foil of Sancho Panza's common sense. In literature, comic effect results whenever flat content is rendered in lofty form. Readers choose sides between Faulkner's Snopes and Sartoris families; readers like heroes and villains even when stereotypes are softened by subtlety, relish the counterpoint between real and fantastic in *The Lord of the Rings,* believe themselves in on the joke when the real England is exaggerated so they view with double vision the strange, yet familiar travels of Lemuel Gulliver. Thanks to Kafka, readers even know how it feels to be treated like a giant insect. Most fiction first sets up a contrast, then amplifies to active conflict by turning up the volume. Tyler moves from death into noisy, hectic life.

But contrasts are not essential to literature alone. An ability to see right through contrast with double vision, perhaps all the way to unity, seems vital to every creative activity. Frozen dilemma produces no forward movement. The process of thesis/antithesis/synthesis, run by verbally at 100 m.p.h., is metaphor—called by Aristotle the one gift that cannot be taught. To think in metaphor is a talent: to superimpose unlike objects and achieve something new so that when Juliet calls Romeo a "beautiful tyrant" we know in the tension between two words what is meant. Kepler's particular talent saw the link between the motions of the tides and the motions of the moon. Creative talent made Pythagoras discover musical harmony while watching blacksmiths hammer iron bars of different lengths while each sounded at a different pitch. With metaphor, one scientist expressed the connection between energy and matter—E equals MC^2—and the gospels depict one long metaphor, "God is love."

But Anne Tyler's metaphorical work, to posit opposites and reconcile some, occurs where more than charity begins, at home, where she has lived as daughter, wife, and mother of two daughters. In her essay, "Still Just Writing,"[3] she specifies antithetical partitions in her own mind that separate the domestic and professional halves of her life. Once, she says, she made the mistake of trying with a tape recorder to capture those wonderful story ideas that came during the buzz of the vacuum cleaner; but the experiment failed because she had violated essential divisions in her life. She decided, then, that her method would be to keep hold of two strings: when she went into her study to write fiction, she needed to drop in the hall the string of her domestic life and pick up the writer's string waiting for her across the threshold. Many working American women will sigh and nod to this household schizophrenia they also live forty-eight hours per day, in a setting where blood certainly *is* thicker than water, even when spilled or sucked. (Evidently Tyler also carries two separate strings for her private and public lives, and rarely picks up the public one.)

Reading about Tyler's strings of identity made me remember 1964, the

5

year she was publishing her first novel, written during her first six months of marriage when, she says (perhaps nostalgically?), she didn't have much else to do. By 1964 our children were aged four, ten, and eleven, and I had far too much to do; so I was famished to find some Handy Dandy Shortcut to writing, any system that would help me spew out twenty pages of prose in about twenty minutes stolen daily time. Published in 1964, besides Tyler's first novel, was Arthur Koestler's *The Act of Creation,* which examines far more cogently than I can the nature of the creative process, suggesting that it occurs—whether for Sophocles or Charlie Chaplin—whenever two unrelated causal chains collide and perhaps merge or reveal something new. Rothenburg has called this simultaneous recognition of opposites "Janusian thinking," after the Roman god Janus, whose two faces point in opposite directions. Our month January is named for his doubleness, facing both New Year and Old, and the two-faced Janus appears on the Dell paperback edition of Koestler's book about oppositions and collisions and syntheses. In a pun, for instance, Koestler says two strings of word-thought get tangled into an acoustic knot. In novels, conflict causes plot, just as in the Chinese language the word "crisis" is composed of two characters—one represents danger, and one represents opportunities. The foundation of quantum physics is also laid on an apparent contradiction between particle and wave images.

So encouraged was I in 1964 by Koestler's analysis that I set out to fuse it with my desperate need to speed the writing process. I would disturb equilibrium by focusing on contrast and thus leap overhead into the "Eureka" of new stories! Toward that end I drew up a long list of apparent polarities. Meditating on youth/age, body/soul, night/day, sweet/sour, life/death would by dynamic tension alone fling high my yin/yang ingredients for cooking up fiction.

The 1964 short stories resulting from this attempt to make my left brain consciously teach "breathing lessons" to my right brain were, as you would expect, terrible.

Though Anne Tyler surely never wasted time compiling such a list nor cooking up fiction after deliberate manichaeanism, criticism of her work usually takes note of its repeated pull between contraries and toward balance. Stella Nesanovich's 1979 LSU dissertation, "The Individual in the Family," could in spots have been "the individual *versus* the family." An earlier article of mine divided Tyler's characters in her first nine novels between stay-at-homes and runaways. "Without contraries," said William Blake, who married Heaven and Hell, "there's no progression."

Even Tyler's titles produce doubling or marry opposites. In *Earthly Possessions,* for instance, one hears the first obvious meaning and then a reversal echo, "What on *earth* possessed you!" The restaurant in her ninth title reminds a reader of how it feels to be simultaneously sick *for* home, and sick *of* home. That cliche, "armchair traveler," gets flipped to the logo on Macon Leary's guidebooks, "traveling armchairs." In fact, the title is nearly an oxymoron—how can a tourist be accidental? Tyler has played with this particular contrast before by featuring the non-tour at the end of *Earthly Possessions* where Charlotte and Saul (like Macon Leary, like Ralph Waldo Emerson) have traveled extensively at home. In fact, Tyler's pilgrimages frequently turn into the one the Queen described to Alice, "It takes all the running you can do to keep in the same place." Her running/staying characters have personalities that also contrast or clash, like Cody with Ezra in one novel or, on a larger scale, Morgan Gower as Jeremy Pauling turned wrongside out. Typical Tyler clashes and mixtures resonate across all eleven novels, in which readers will recognize similar names, situations, cardgames, prodigal fathers, funerals, kidnaps and near-kidnaps—the same elements stirred and restirred. The portrait painter Sir Joshua Reynolds was famous for the subtle tones he achieved in flesh and fabric, and when asked, "What do you mix your colors with?" replied quickly, "brains." As Tyler's novels accumulate, her mixtures also grow more subtle, her sketches of individual families widen into murals of the human family.

The title of her Pulitzer prize-winning novel blends an action that is reflexive, autonomic, natural—"breathing"—with a process deliberate, cerebral, learned—"lessons."

Keeping in mind Ben Jonson's claim that "all concord's born of contraries," look more closely at how Tyler marries opposites in *Breathing Lessons,* so printed by Knopf that when the reader flips through the book its pages will alternate subliminally, with the word "breathing" printed atop each lefthand page, "lessons" atop the right.

First, examine the dustjacket on the hardcover edition, a painting Anne Tyler approved, by New York artist Tom Woodruff. Its interlocking circles certainly suggest the eternal rings of double wedding bands and bonds, but these particular circles have been formed by midair birds in flight, perhaps shortlived sparrows like those which in Jesus' time were sold for a farthing and thus symbolized brief, anonymous life, though He said the Heavenly Father noticed each one. In *her* created world, Anne Tyler also seems to notice every sparrow-gray character, those who fly and those who fall.

Below these birds-of-a-feather flying on the cover runs a small road with double ruts that "rise to converge" on the horizon. This overall scene with golden light emanating on all sides was suggested to the painter by that moment in the novel when Maggie and Ira Moran scare up birds as they drive along the road. Whatever has sent them into air, these wild birds have superimposed themselves into a pair of almost harmonious circles—I say "almost" because in Tyler's world one or two birds are always loose from the flock.

This cover illustration, like a ghost picture on the reader's retina, overlays

Chapter 1 in which Maggie Moran hears on her car radio a call-in broadcast on the topic of ideal marriage. After twenty-eight years Maggie, 48, and her husband Ira, 50, have not an ideal but a *real* marriage, warts and all; but what their son Jessie has is a broken one. Though Maggie knows what the Swiss say, that "marriage is a covered dish," she so often hears what she wants to hear that on this Saturday morning she is convinced that one radio caller's voice belongs to Jesse's divorced wife Fiona, announcing on the air that having once married for true love she will now do the opposite and remarry for security. Shocked, Maggie immediately hits the accelerator instead of the brake and while locked in this opposition is herself hit by a Pepsi-Cola truck.

With that opening moment of start/stop/collision, while the air is full of broadcast news of an old and new marriage, in the context of an upcoming funeral to be conducted like a renewal of wedding vows, Tyler begins this journey which will cluster her contrasts in a single day.

Her plot seems simple, since Tyler's plots are usually means to her ends of revealing character and theme. This time her main characters have grown older, the marriage and conflict are longer lived. Maggie Moran is 48, as Tyler was in October of 1989—not that life begins at middle-age, but that's where it does begin to show. If in middle age you try on a bathing suit in front of a floor length mirror, you realize that "skin tight" isn't that accurate a description. It's certainly the right age for a Janus view, remembering the past, looking with some anxiety toward the future.

Part I, told from Maggie's middle-aged point of view, contains three chapters. The first provides context for the Moran family: Maggie and Ira, Jesse and Fiona, and their daughter Leroy. Chapter 2, the self-contained portion excerpted by *The New Yorker,* moves the Moran couple ninety miles north of Baltimore to the funeral of Max Gill (Gill is not, ah, breathing anymore) in Deer Lick, Pa. These last rites have been planned by his widow Serena Gill as a reenactment of their nuptial rites, complete with pop love songs to be resung by aging friends from the original wedding party who, like Maggie, have not just *kept* their youthful figures but doubled them.

Chapter 3 describes the wake at Serena Gill's home, during which silent home movies will be shown depicting the corpse as bridegroom a quarter century ago. During this event, which brings alive neither Gill nor the Sixties, Ira and Maggie slip upstairs and counteract death by enjoying spontaneous sex in the dead man's bedroom.

Part II, almost a separate story, is only fifty pages long, the only section narrated by Ira, and again almost a sandwich filling between thicker slices of "what Maggie knows." Headed home from Gill's funeral, Maggie, annoyed by a bad driver, yells at him that his wheel is loose. She is stricken when the driver, Daniel Otis, believes her lie and also turns out to be both old and black, a double assault on her conscience since good-hearted Maggie works with the aged in a rest home. Mr. Otis becomes one more stray person Maggie keeps inviting into their lives; Ira sees this incident and their involvement with the Otis family as a hyperbolic expansion on her earlier instant intimacy with a waitress in a roadside cafe.

In Part III, four chapters through Maggie's point of view, her Good Samaritanism becomes even more fullblown, though not every injured neighbor proves grateful. The long marriage of Ira and Maggie is contrasted with the brief marriage of Jesse and Fiona seven years earlier; both of these form a contrast with the "ideal marriage" broadcast into the Platonic ether in Chapter 1. If the first marriage evolved into a wedlock in which two different people have learned to live as partners, the second turned into a deadlock from which Jesse and Fiona escaped. Maggie, who once believed marriage would be "an alteration in people's lives, two opposites drawn together with a dramatic crashing sound" (BL 246) now understands that every individual problem of the bride and groom will persist afterward, become entwined, perhaps even synthesize.

In Part III, Ira and Maggie, still headed home from the funeral, take the detour Maggie demands to invite Fiona and Leroy home to Baltimore overnight. Once Maggie has them under her roof she begins her old efforts to turn white lies into bandages, trying unsuccessfully to bring Jesse back home as well. She, not they, will tie their marriage bond again. A meddler, a unifier, an improver, Friedrich Hegel in an apron, Maggie sees the world "out of focus, the colors not within the lines" (BL 312), and still believes that if she could only make a correcting adjustment then "everything would settle perfectly into place" (BL 312).

During the domestic conflicts that result, Maggie relives her early days as mother-in-law. By then she had already acted out Samuel Butler's remark, "Life is like playing a violin solo in public and learning the instrument as one goes on," and she wanted Jesse and Fiona to master her particular epithalamion. Literally the "breathing lessons" learned were those Maggie helped Fiona practice when she was pregnant with Leroy. Now at 48, Maggie is certain that everybody's childhood lessons in piano playing, typing, equations, driving—none of these provided training in the skills needed for "living day in and day out with a husband and raising up a new human being" (BL 182). Maggie makes readers recall that moment post partum, when nurses shooed them into a car and placed a strange and fragile baby in their laps. "If I'm a parent," everyone thinks at that time, "they must have lowered the requirements."

In his own way, Jesse did try to master those requirements seven years earlier. As an expectant father, he devoured baby books (Jeremy Pauling also read up on fatherhood), believing, like many Americans males, that "reading up, getting equipped" would put him in control. But despite book lessons, Jesse has become one more failed amateur at marriage and fa-

9

therhood. Ira thinks him a failure as a son as well. For all her clumsy, sometimes misguided meddling, Maggie could not "teach" him and Fiona then, nor on this day seven years later, the lessons that "real life" has slowly imparted to her in the School of Hard Knocks. Nor has she herself learned every other would-be teacher's lesson. She rejected the one taught by Ira's embittered father Sam, for example. She has remained deaf to the sad instruction of seniors in the rest home where she works, whose lives are worn beyond repair. She has not lowered her sights to the level from which commonsense Ira views the world.

Ira's diagnosis is that since Maggie believes the people she loves are better than they are, she changes reality to suit her view of them—a charge also implied against Anne Tyler as author by Edward Hoagland in his *New York Times* review of *Breathing Lessons*. Tyler is "not unblinking," he writes; she skips over racial friction even though it regularly occurs in the very Baltimore neighborhoods she writes about. In all eleven Tyler novels, he says, "Her people are eerily virtuous, Quakerishly tolerant of all strangers, all races. And she touches upon sex so lightly, compared with her graphic realism on other matters, that her total portrait of motivation is tilted out of balance."[4]

Some might argue that Hoagland's view of sex as prime mover is influenced by his gender, but Tyler draws complaints from militant feminist readers as well. Her focus on family may shortchange unmarried, divorced, childless or single-parent career women as heroines and as a reading audience. Other feminists frown over that scene in *Breathing Lessons* where Maggie rushes to the clinic to persuade Fiona not to go through with her planned abortion. Though Tyler's description of pro-lifers who are demonstrating angrily at curbside hardly seems sympathetic, some pro-choice readers want to be sure which of Maggie's anti-abortion arguments belong to Maggie and which belong to Tyler. One might as well insist that *Sense and Sensibility* take a stand on Napoleon, that *Emma* be more forceful about the War of 1812, or that *Persuasion* concern itself with the 1817 riots in Derbyshire over low wages.

Reading audiences do change, however, and if Jane Austen's novels develop toward final marriages, it may be less persuasive to reconcile plots that same way in 1989—ending as *Earthly Possessions* and *Breathing Lessons* do in the marital bed. In the latter ending, Ira is still awake and at a complex stage of his solitaire game, symbolizing his approach to life; Maggie has just kissed him before getting a good night's sleep so she'll be ready to travel on tomorrow, symbolizing hers.

What about the other endings to Tyler's novels? Are they unblinking, feminist? Do they constitute a synthesis arrived at after the clashing of opposites? What kind of synthesis?

At the end of *The Tin Can Tree*, P.J. climbs into the car and falls asleep with her head on Peter's lap. In *Earthly Possessions,* Saul and Charlotte in the old sleigh bed decide not to take a trip because their lives are the trip. "Go to sleep," says Charlotte, and he does—a small reversal of who has the insomnia from *Breathing Lessons.* A much older Miss Vinton has the last word of *Celestial Navigation,* looking at herself and Jeremy Pauling as they must appear to the eyes of a lighthearted whistling boy, who sees them as not at all star-crossed, just an elderly couple at the end of the dusty and unremarkable journey of their lives. *Dinner at the Homesick Restaurant* ends as Cody leads Beck back toward the family meal, the funeral meats. In *The Accidental Tourist* Macon is leaping from his Paris taxicab because Muriel is waiting by the curb, just as Morgan Gower (*Morgan's Passing*) starts humming while he walks toward another curb where Emily holds Josh on one hip. No rebellious Nora goes slamming out of her doll's house in these conclusions; no woman is swimming out to where horizon meets sea or going mad from seeing creatures swarm inside her yellow wallpaper.

Yet Tyler's reconciliations must not be made to seem as easy as Blondie's with Dagwood; she knows these risks. In *Morgan's Passing,* the puppet show does not end with the beast changing into a prince because "we use a more authentic version" (83). And usually Tyler presents opposing views, as through Sarah Leary, whose reaction to her son's murder is to decide that life is meaningless, and human beings evil. It would not suit the tone and purpose of *Breathing Lessons* to conduct marital conflict at the level of Medea vs. Jason, yet Tyler does catalogue those maddening habits of men and women which drive husbands and wives crazy. She even dares make almost stereotyped assumptions about gender roles in America: Ira is too quiet and self-contained; disorganized Maggie confides in absolute strangers. Don't most T.V. sitcoms also pair the impetuous meddling female with a patient, less excitable male? When Maggie storms out of the car and threatens to leave him forever, Ira does drive away and stay away just long enough to fill one episode. In his taciturn Gary Cooper way he says in the final moments of *Breathing Lessons,* "Maggie, honey" (*BL* 314) or "There, now, sweetheart" (*BL* 326). After twenty-eight years of rehearsal, the Moran disagreements have taken on the skills, stratagems, and compromises superficially sketched on the Cosby Show, but a novelist can enter her characters' minds, not just their apartments, and characters can read one another's thoughts. Maggie, for example, understands Ira's mood by the tune he whistles. (Tyler's father did this kind of whistling.)

Like other Tyler characters, the Morans are amazed at how their lives have turned out. Even Ira's marriage proposal seems an accidental byproduct of a quarrel with his father, while Maggie's bridal candidacy resulted from a mistake she made about which soldier was dead. She considers Jesse's and Fiona's divorce almost accidental as well, the result of missed communications. The Morans live out their amazement at unpredictable life in ways associated with standard male/female attitudes: Maggie still busily trying to tinker with and repair life, Ira meditating more abstractly on the wastes of mortality and time. During his brief narration, Ira achieves the theme of "Our Town," through one of his periodic insights into how much he loves his awkward, lopsided, transitory family, whether he tells them out loud or not. His other half, Maggie, already knows she loves hers, tells them, and also wants to darn their lives, like socks. Unlike feminist writers who have mocked gender roles, or who have made marriage a battlefield between the sexes, Tyler carries sexual stereotypes to deeper, more complex levels to attempt in fiction what Josef Albers aspires to in his painting, "to make black and white behave together instead of shooting at each other only."

What I have called Tyler's use of thesis/antithesis/synthesis becomes for Mary F. Robertson in *Contemporary American Women Writers* a pattern of strangers disrupting a family's ordered life, then altering it into something new.[5] One possible dissenter to us both is John Updike, obviously a Tyler admirer, who nonetheless complains of one weakness: "a tendency to leave the reader just where she found him."[6] Updike believes the ends of Tyler's novels have *not* actually moved far from their beginning pages into new syntheses. Charlotte, after all, is back home with Saul; Jeremy ends up at home with a substitute wife/mother; Beck has come home to the dinner table even if he insists he'll leave again before the wine is poured; and, in *Breathing Lessons,* Maggie is going to sleep on her side of the bed much as she must have gone to sleep the Friday night before the novel opened on Saturday morning.

In Tyler's fiction, the marriage of opposites does not produce radically different offspring. The real adventure is not to light out for the territory with Huck Finn but to function as the Hallmark card advises, even with all the risks of sentimentality that affirmation entails, to "Bloom where you are planted." Some find her developing work to be more positive than realism warrants. It is said that Tyler only chooses to review those books she expects to like, and in fiction, too, she seldom lingers long on characters who are actively mean spirited.

But in his *Times* review, though Hoagland finds her "Quakerish," he does not call Tyler's themes sentimental but links her with Henry James. Both, he says, produce a "literature of resignation—of wisely settling for less than life had seemed to offer . . . a theme more European than New World by tradition." Such a theme, Hoagland thinks, is now coming into its own with the "graying of America into middle age since World War II."[7]

No one is more aware than Tyler of the risks either of boring compromise on the one hand or—worse for us women writers—sentimentality on the other, in such resignation. One slip of her pen and certain Tyler characters might begin warbling, "Brighten the corner where you are," or quoting Edgar Guest, "it takes a heap o' living/to make a house a home" or—as

Maggie sometimes does in *Breathing Lessons*—exhibiting too predictable a mixture of tenderhearted with madcap-cute, like Lucille Ball. I agree with critic Joseph Voelker that sometimes Tyler casts on Maggie Moran an eye almost as cool as Graham Greene in *The Heart of the Matter* casts upon Scobie, though the issues are much smaller.[8] And I prefer *Celestial Navigation* and *Dinner at the Homesick Restaurant* precisely because the issues are larger, the opposites more distinct, the ambiguities in their resolution more persistent. But many of Tyler's most devoted readers would disagree, would even claim that Maggie's outlook on life duplicates her creator's.

Nor do I want to be counted with those critics who object to Tyler's fiction *because* her work aims steadily at reconciliation. William Gass once remarked that the Pulitzer Prize traditionally went to mediocre talent, an opinion that underscores his own preference for stylistic experiment. Those who prefer experimental work have a temperamental distaste for Tyler's content, her emphasis on life-as-journey, her mature willingness to accept and absorb conflict, her characters' decisions not to seek finality so much as the will to enter tomorrow still doing what one song advises breezily in two novels, "Keep on Truckin'." Some contemporary critics will break out in allergic hives at any literary content containing the slightest histamine of didacticism, affirmation of life, positive thinking.

But Tyler's positivism has more of the tough realism that underlies Madeleine L'Engle's essay about her very old and very ill mother, about the importance of loving her still, loving her enough "to accept her as she is, now, for as long as this dwindling may take."[9]

Quiet acceptance need not minimize the hardships of life, death and despair. In much of her work Tyler has permitted death and despair to intrude, but not to win.

Leslie Fiedler's famous essay about shouting "No, in thunder!"[10] against life's chaos and its daily grind, despair at its brevity and fury over the pious banality of society's advice to cope, seems to assume that to *see* the abyss is automatically to scream at it; to assume that those others who may see it, look down, then turn away silently and get on with the necessities of living are bound to be less sensitive, more superficial, even blind. Women often consider his a romantic, luxury view—available to those who've always had the option of knighthood, war, shipping out on whalers or to the French Foreign Legion, but partially foreclosed, say, for Emily Dickinson, who could only climb the stairs. For those left home to nurse the old folks through their long vomits of fatal cancer, shouting "no" would get no bedpans emptied. Tyler's feminism is of this less dramatic sort—she admires the people, often women, who have an abyss running right through their own backyards and still hang out the laundry.

Anne Tyler depicts the non-shouters, those people who "go on meaning well," ordinary people who seem "funny and strange to me, and touching in unexpected ways. I can't shake off," she says "a sort of mist of irony that hangs over whatever I see."[11]

So *The Accidental Tourist* opens in the rain as *A Farewell to Arms* closes in the rain. And if a denouement is usually the point in fiction that *un*ravels the tangles in story plot, consider for contrast the spontaneous *du*et of Ira and Maggie which is joined in the supermarket, their voices after much disagreement still plaited, braided. At the end of *Breathing Lessons* Ira stops Maggie's latest scheme to bring Leroy to live with them and brighten her own future days as well as his by enrolling in the superior Baltimore schools. Ira stops her by saying, "'Maggie, look at me.' She faced him, hands on her hips. 'No,' he said" (326).

Contrast Ira Moran's not very thunderous "No" with what happens in the end of that ultimate pop novel, *Gone With the Wind*, a novel Leslie Fiedler calls part of our national myth, as "southern" as our movies are sometimes "western." Many male writers would end that novel with a "no," at least in moderate thunder, by stopping where Rhett Butler says, "Frankly, my dear, I don't give a damn," and departs. In fact, thousands of readers (who have not been polled by gender) remember both book and film as ending exactly on that note.

But Margaret Mitchell (who called herself "a dynamo going to waste") ended her only novel in the same tone Tyler's chief characters in her also popular novels stubbornly employ. "Tomorrow will be better," thinks Scarlet O'Hara at the end of *Gone with the Wind*, just as Maggie Moran— stopped by circumstances, stopped by her husband's firm "No"—may seem to drift into sleep acquiescent although the previous 325 pages have made clear that for Maggie, too, tomorrow will always be a new day. Even in dreams she will be scheming up ways to use tomorrow, to improve the ordinary people living there and remold them nearer to the heart's desire. It is as if, with Tyler's women, indeed with many heroines at the end of novels by women, the closing mood is: "And that's semi-final!"

In her long consideration about opposites and how they marry, after eleven novels about love, home, family, and survival, *Breathing Lessons* is surely semi-final, and Anne Tyler is already dreaming up Novel Number 12.

NOTES

1. Carl Schoettler, "New Anne Tyler Novel Magnifies the Mundane" [rev. of *Breathing Lessons*], *The [Baltimore] Evening Sun*, 1 September 1988, sec. D, p. 1.

2. "Anne Tyler," *Dictionary of Literary Biography*, vol. 6: *American Novelists since World War II, Second Series*, ed. James E. Kibler, Jr. (Detroit: Gale Research, 1980), p. 337.

3. In *The Writer on Her Work*, ed. Janet Sternburg (New York: Norton, 1980), p. 9.

4. "About Maggie, Who Tried Too Hard," *The New York Times Book Review*, 11 September 1988, p. 44.

5. "Anne Tyler: Medusa Points and Contact Points," in *Contemporary American Women Writers: Narrative Strategies,* ed. Catherine Rainwater and William J. Scheick (Lexington: University Press of Kentucky, 1985), pp. 119–142.

6. "Loosened Roots" [rev. of *Earthly Possessions*], *The New Yorker,* 53 (6 June 1977), 130.

7. "About Maggie, Who Tried Too Hard," p. 44.

8. A remark made by Joseph C. Voelker in an open forum at the Anne Tyler Symposium, Baltimore, April, 1989.

9. *The Summer of the Great Grandmother* (San Francisco: Harper & Row, 1974, 1979), p. 149.

10. "The Power of Blackness: Faustian Man and the Cult of Violence," in *Love and Death in the American Novel,* rev. ed. (New York: Dell, 1960, 1966), p. 505.

11. "Still Just Writing," in *The Writer on Her Work,* p. 12.

The Nature of Kinship
in the Novels of Anne Tyler

VIRGINIA SCHAEFER CARROLL

O ne of the distinctive features of many of Tyler's novels is the intricate development and revelation of the central characters' complex family structures. As one moves through the homes of families like the Hawkeses, the Paulings, the Emersons, the Pecks, the Morans, the Tulls, and the Learys, one finds a recurrent theme: the presentation of kinship as both a nurturing bond and a source of isolation for the individual. Although the settings are contemporary, the plots contain recognizable elements of primitive structures. It does not matter that the residents at the Paulings' home sit in the glow of the television instead of the tribal fire, that the Leary, Moran, and Emerson families are characterized, in part, by the way they drive automobiles: the rituals, the defining of family and clan, the coded language and gestures all suggest a modern, fictive reworking of a fundamental human situation, the ways in which people are drawn to and limited by the need to feel at home.

From this anthropological perspective, one of the first points to make about Tyler's work is that often the novels present groups which resemble clans rather than families. Families are biogenetically linked groups in which identity is based on similarities in genes, temperament, build, and habits.[1] Certainly one sees this kind of link when Elizabeth Abbot recognizes even in Peter, the alienated son in *The Clock Winder*, irrefutable evidence of his genealogy, and mumbles to herself, "Emersons" (*CW* 310). One sees it in *The Accidental Tourist* when the wives roll their eyes and "go on and on about the Leary men" (*AT* 14). One sees this biogenetic similarity

16

even in Jesse Moran's expression, as he holds "his face in a way that caused his chin to lengthen, just as Ira always did when he was trying to keep back a smile" (*BL* 307). But in many cases, the families in Tyler's novels are linked according to the ties which Bronislaw Malinowski identifies as peculiar to clans: unlike the domestic institution of the family, the clan is based on "mythological fictions of a unilateral common descent from an ancestor or ancestress."[2] This kind of kinship is totemic in nature and is unified through a series of mysterious duties.

In many of Tyler's novels, the absence of a family member through death, separation, or desertion hollows out the core of strong biogenetic relationships. In its place is a modern mythology which the characters invent for themselves: Caleb, missing for over sixty years, is sought as the key to understanding and unifying the Peck family; the invented, haunting reconstruction of Beck Tull is stronger than the actual man who shares a table with his family at the Homesick Restaurant; and Ethan Leary, who appears in Macon's dreams as a twelve-year-old, bouncing lightly on the balls of his feet, remains a mythologized force in the lives of his parents. Other mythologies are invented as well, including the very sense of home and security that permeates most of the works. Even in Tyler's first novel, *If Morning Ever Comes,* Ben Joe Hawkes shuffles with his suitcase through the halls of his family's home, lured by the familiar sounds of arguments over gin rummy and the reading aloud of *Winnie-the-Pooh.* He struggles with this self-limited view of his family in a frozen moment, framed like the warm yellow square of sunlight in the long front hall, as opposed to the boundless dark nights when he feels alienated from his sisters, who pad by his door in their slippers. Like many of Tyler's characters, Ben Joe must wrestle with the fact that the kinship he feels is based on a wholly fictive, ideal sense of his family and his position in it.

One of the strongest appeals of Tyler's fiction, however, is the revelation of these mythological relationships. By repeatedly showing each family's response to outsiders, Tyler allows the reader to see how modern American families (partly, perhaps, to compensate for the missing biological links) construct identity through rituals and symbols and allow access only to those who have proven themselves worthy of trust, respect, and initiation. In *Searching for Caleb,* for example, one finds that the gypsy nature of the Peck family is checked by their fear of wandering, of blending into others. As Anne G. Jones points out, the Pecks are extremely careful about their connections with others:

[They] have isolated themselves for five generations by stiffly valuing the virtues of politeness, suppression of feeling, and submersion of idiosyncrasy. Their credo is "avoid the new": they have roped in outside genes for reproduction, but then driven the breeders—Margaret Rose, Sam Mayhew—away.[3]

Their attitude about outsiders seems harsh, but Claude Levi-Strauss, in *The Elementary Structures of Kinship,* explains that across cultures, all rights are determined by kinship: all who are kin or resemble one's kin are irrationally trusted, all others mistrusted and seen as potential enemies.[4] Here as in other novels, the spouses of the clan never quite transcend the label of *outsider.* Although the Pecks—with the notable exception of the married cousins, Duncan and Justine—see exogamy as necessary for procreative purposes, it is unsatisfying in the mythological sense of kinship and self-sufficiency which they have established for themselves.

The Tulls are similarly frustrated in their attempts to reconcile their views of home and their real lives. Doris Betts states that the Homesick Restaurant "expresses Tyler's usual paradox: sick FOR home, sick OF home."[5] The fact that the action builds to a scene in a restaurant is critical, however. As Julian Pitt-Rivers explains, "the first social criterion of a common humanity is to be able to eat the same food."[6] In this novel, nevertheless, one of the most basic bonding rituals—sharing a meal—becomes a source of conflict and confusion. The reunion between the grown children and their long-absent father is disappointing, for ultimately he is a stranger whose respect and approval mean very little when actually seen on his face. Tyler summarizes his reception in these few lines: to those gathered at the dinner, Beck was seen " . . . as a brand-new chance—a fresh start, someone to appreciate them at last. Yet when they finally sat down, no one chose a place near Beck." (*DHR* 290–91)

In *Celestial Navigation,* Tyler introduces the Paulings on the basis of their kinship. Amanda worries that Jeremy, whom she identifies as her "last blood relation" (*CN* 7), is irrevocably entrenched in the absurd rituals of the family from which she escaped. Her own meticulousness, planning, and lack of sensitivity, however, seem to be only a mutant strain of the same affliction that forces Mrs. Pauling and Jeremy to the opposite extreme. Mary Tell, on the other hand, represents an entirely different force. She is not a family member like Amanda or Laura, who, although occasionally exasperated by Jeremy, always accept him on his own terms. Mary is immediately defined as a stranger to Jeremy. She says, "He makes me feel too tall and too loud and too strong. I never know how to act with him." (*CN* 62) Their courtship consists of a series of conversations in which their messages are misunderstood: Mary assumes he wants the rent money when he calls at her door with flowers, and Jeremy absentmindedly eats the stale, melting chocolates he had ventured all the way to the grocery store to find for her.

Their first intimacy—exchanging first names—is also awkward, a clumsy exchange that presents itself as a hurdle instead of a joy. But the effects of Mary Tell's presence show that even Jeremy Pauling understands the need to bond with another human being beyond his closed, clutter-filled circle.

18

He sees his love for Mary as a "suicidal leap into unknown waters" (*CN* 88), a rushing toward the edge of some "high cliff" (*CN* 90); but the reader sees, for a very short space, a life in Jeremy that is evident in no other part of the work. Even his devotion to his art is apparently without passion. Mary brings him out of himself for a while: he moves beyond the threshold where his mother died, and he symbolically dons a pen-and-pencil set in his pocket as a self-proclaimed "sign of competence" (*CN* 98). Ultimately, however, this bonding with the outsider is very short lived. Although he claims that "he could follow Mary all the way off his island" (*CN* 104) and that he is "slaying dragons" (*CN* 108) for her, crossing the street makes him recoil and ask, "How would he ever get home again?" (*CN* 109–10) Mary's inevitable abandonment of him, as he isolates himself in his studio, is both tragic and inconsequential to him. Jeremy's art represents the abstract, mythologized sense of family which he prefers:

> . . . in Jeremy's piece, there were no people. Only the *feeling* of people—of full lives suddenly interrupted, belongings still bearing the imprint of their vanished owners. Dark squares upstairs full of toys, paper scraps, a plastic doll bed lying on its side as if some burst of exuberance had flung it there and then moved on, leaving such a vacancy it could make you cry. (*CN* 246)

Jeremy protects himself from outsiders, particularly Mary, by clinging fiercely to the identity given to him by his mother—the view of himself as a gifted artist, capable of rendering scraps into art that he values little.

In *The Accidental Tourist,* Macon Leary's writing represents a similar kind of art, for he pieces together insignificant facts—where one can find homogenized milk or a king-sized Beautyrest mattress—into collages that others find useful and even inspiring. But he, a tourist who only passes through much of his personal life, longs for the mythologized sense of home which underlies his travel guides. More than any other of Tyler's characters, Macon Leary has a totemic view of the world and especially of strangers: on a plane, the man with the headset is safe; the woman with the Life Savers and afghan is not (*AT* 30–31). He himself is represented by *Miss MacIntosh,* the Macon Leary Body Bag, a winged armchair. The baked potato is the totem which links Macon with Porter, Charles, and Rose; like all totems, it is both a concrete and metaphorical way of representing common identity, in this case the preference for comfort and blandness.[7] And a glimpse at Tyler's puns about the family shows that they also share similar views of outsiders: being leery is synonymous with being a Leary; Julian will probably always be considered an Edge.

This bond of blood, when tested, proves itself stronger than any other in *The Accidental Tourist,* consistent with David Schneider's assertion that "kinship consists in bonds on which kinsmen can depend and which are compelling and stronger than, and take priority over, other kinds of bonds."[8] For example, when Rose calls to console Macon on his separation from Sarah, he makes clear that he expects Rose to be loyal to her blood, not to her gender. And she is. Despite the fact that Rose states, matter of factly, "Everybody knows the Leary men are difficult to live with" (*AT* 13), she clearly allies herself with her brother when they move to defend a family ritual which was once under attack by the spouses: the use of alphabetized lists. The narrator cannot refrain from inserting this ironic comment: "Rose had a kitchen that was so completely alphabetized, you'd find the allspice next to the ant poison. She was a fine one to talk about the Leary men." (*AT* 14) The Leary clan share a devotion to the laws of logic, vaccination, and grammar. Few but the Learys would pause to engage in a serious discussion of primitive and modern food-gathering; and only the Learys would conclude that, as people bring in bags of groceries, domesticated animals must view them as "the greatest hunters on earth" (*AT* 63). Almost from birth lacking the stability of a biogenetic family, the Learys share a strong need to perform the rituals of their clan.

Their alienation from outsiders is portrayed as both comic and sad. Porter, now divorced, would rather clean out the gutters with his children than try to choose a restaurant with them; Rose would rather cook for "the boys" than stay with her husband Julian. Macon's bewildering encounters with outsiders provide the action of much of this novel. He preserves his own and his family's identity through limited contact with others, and he always sees the alien as a threat: "Physical contact with people not related to him—an arm around his shoulder, a hand on his sleeve—made him draw inward like a snail" (*AT* 48). He even defines those outside his family as somehow outside of humanity, stating that "outsiders' skin felt so unreal" (*AT* 48) and that his idea of hell is a shopping mall, "with all those strangers' shoulders brushing his" (*AT* 49).

His marriage to Sarah and his involvement with Muriel Pritchett—people also not related to him—arouse similar feelings of dread. Although Sarah is necessary in the creation of Ethan, whom he recognizes as a Leary after all, her feelings, responses to crises, and even her language remain alien to him. She closes her letters with "I love you," he with "fondly" (*AT* 51); when, in the depths of grief, she fantasizes about shooting their son's murderer, he tells her, "It's not productive" (*AT* 24). He even begins to view her "as a form of enemy" (*AT* 68) when scrutinized from the safe distance of his family home. Muriel, too, is immediately labeled as an outsider, a woman whose hair "burgeoned to her shoulders like an Arab headdress" (*AT* 28), and whose mannerisms and language are no less exotic.

The irony and charm of Macon's stance toward these women is that he is unsure of his own rightful position toward them. Lying in bed after his accident, he is pleased by the easy familiarity of the family sounds that waft to his bedroom. When his brothers return from work, the atmosphere is "relieved, relaxed" (*AT* 76), and he telescopes his entire marriage—his time away from them—as a "brief trip elsewhere" (*AT* 76). Yet, while playing cards in the evening, Macon is brought to a moment of crisis. Glancing at their childhood portraits and at their current images reflected in panes of glass, Macon is terrified at the thought of remaining forever fixed in the same place, of allowing no one in. That moment of self-recognition allows him to go beyond his kin once again. And in his longest speech of the novel, the moment of vulnerability when Macon allows Muriel to hold him and listen to what it means to "experience . . . a loss" (*AT* 199), Macon's description of his life, his marriage, his grieving all builds to this revealing final line: "And now I'm far removed from everyone: I don't have friends anymore and everyone looks trivial and foolish and not related to me" (*AT* 200). Muriel recognizes his need to be taken in, to be rescued, and to be reassured, "You are not the only one" (*AT* 201).

Maggie Moran, in *Breathing Lessons,* feels a strong urge to rescue her own family members through direct manipulation and mythologizing. Like Pearl Tull, who makes each new house "airtight and rustproof and waterproof" (*DHR* 16) and Pamela Emerson, who frets that her house may not be sealed against invading locusts, Maggie uses her own tools to insulate and protect her home. In this novel, however, in which much of the action occurs on a trip, home is much more abstract and takes considerably more work to hold together. For example, although the narrator states in the first chapter that "Maggie couldn't care less what made an ideal marriage" (*BL* 5), much of the novel's action revolves around Maggie's shock to think that Fiona might be "marrying some total stranger purely for security" (*BL* 7). Labeled by one reviewer as a meddler, an "incorrigible prompter,"[9] Maggie frenetically pulls together her family in response to her fears of society, aging, and change.

Her concern is not only to protect those she loves but also to preserve a sense of herself that is somehow incomplete. After the accident in which she has accelerated instead of braked—symbolic of a much deeper instinct—she explains this fear to Ira: "I feel like we're just flying apart! All my friends and relatives just flying off from me like the . . . expanding universe or something!" (*BL* 10) To hold her kin together, Maggie becomes fiercely devoted to people she seems not even to like. She defends Jesse but actually feels exasperation with him through most of the work. She wants to keep Daisy away from "Mrs. Perfect" but actually feels more pain than joy when her daughter is home. She is devoted to the *idea* of Leroy but is disappointed that "there wasn't a trace of Jesse in that child's appearance" (*BL* 188). Her brief attempt at conversation with the seven-year-old leaves Maggie "spent, wondering where to go from there" (*BL* 190).

As usual, when Maggie is confronted by glaring reality, she concocts a myth to bind the family together and to reassure herself that nothing is flying apart. It was, after all, an overstated letter and a song that united her with Ira years before. Her invention about Jesse's building a cradle once succeeded in pulling Fiona to her son. She thus builds a binding story about Fiona's soapbox in order to lure her back to Baltimore:

> The day you left, that evening, I found Jesse in the bedroom with his nose buried deep in your soapbox and his eyes closed. . . . I believe he has kept that soapbox to this day, Fiona, and you can't tell me it's because he feels sorry for you. He wants to remember you. He goes by smell, just the way I do; smell is what brings a person most clearly to his mind. (*BL* 206)

Her use of the qualifier, "I believe," is not only her means of avoiding an outright lie; it is also a statement of her creed. She would like to believe that Jesse longs for Fiona's return. And until Ira sabotages her efforts by pointing out that Jesse sleeps with an auto greeter, not a soapbox (*BL* 309), Maggie's plan works.

Her inventions follow a pattern of blended myth-making and oral history which Levi-Strauss identifies across cultures:

> Of this history that is common in principle, if not always in fact, each family would retain only fragments, and to fill the gaps would borrow from the others, while imposing its own perspective, events analogous to those in which, or so it believed, its members had formerly participated. Thus would be constituted, as the raw material of history, what one could call type-events that are not rigorously true, but are not entirely false either.[10]

Although the characters in the novel see Maggie as lying and misguided, Levi-Strauss' comment suggests a more universal motivation for this kind of behavior. She is reshaping and mythologizing family history to protect them from outsiders.

The most extensive treatment of the theme of the outsider and the clan, however, appears in *The Clock Winder*. The Emersons are no less clannish than the Learys, even though the children are grown and fairly distant as the novel opens. The family is symbolized in one of the first descriptions of the Emerson house: it "was full of clocks, one to a room . . . . Their striking was beautifully synchronized, but the winding was not" (*CW* 7). The connections between the family members—like Mr. Emerson's mysterious system of winding all the clocks—are now unclear, as if the explanation died with the patriarch himself. Some clock winder is needed—someone who, although outside the Emerson clan, accepts any invitation to tinker with the inner workings of a family. Elizabeth Abbot is a threatening necessity to the Emersons.

In the early chapters of the novel, Tyler's descriptions of the Emersons correspond almost directly to Malinowski's definition of a clan. The common ancestor, Mr. Emerson, is mythologized as someone who "knew the answers to questions . . . [Mrs. Emerson] had never thought of asking" (*CW* 8), and the children are connected to their mother only as spokes "moving away from . . . the center of an asterisk" (*CW* 18). The Emersons all have "the same stunned, pale eyes" (*CW* 132), nervous dispositions, and propensity for crises. Their communication and eating rituals clearly distinguish them from the outsiders in the home. Mrs. Emerson murmurs into a Dictaphone messages that only her children will decipher: " 'Everyone knows I am not the sort of mother who interferes.' 'Where is that necklace I lent you?' . . . 'Do you have Emily Barrett's address?' 'Someday *you* will be alone' " (*CW* 36). And Alvareen is clearly amused to hear Elizabeth describe a meal served by Mrs. Emerson: tuna with mushrooms on saltines and celery stalks with oleo and olives.

The Emersons are described as "a bustling foreign tribe" (*CW* 117) who mistrust an alien in their home. Timothy, however charmed by Elizabeth's ease and confidence, feels suddenly protective of his mother and their home. When his car skids into a snowbank, his fear is not only of death, but—worse yet—death "with somebody foreign, not even related to him" (*CW* 75). In a terrible sense, his fear is justified. Elizabeth completely misinterprets his coded language in the moments before his suicide. Her alienation is intensified at the funeral where she looks "out of place, like any ordinary stranger who had stumbled into the midst of a family in mourning" (*CW* 108); Mary, meeting her for the first time, is compelled to ask, "Is that girl all *right?*" (*CW* 126).

Much of the rest of *The Clock Winder* traces Elizabeth's gradual initiation into the Emerson clan. Her response to Timothy's death—an unsatisfying retreat to her own peculiar family—illustrates the danger of living within the limitations of any clan, and Elizabeth comes to realize the need for societal exchanges: she needs to fix things, and the Emersons' house and lives are in disrepair.

In several ways this role is appropriate for an initiate. First, she is an "apprentice," Margaret Morganroth Gullette suggests, because "fixing things prepares her to learn that she can get involved in the real world, risking real disaster."[11] Second, she becomes intimately involved with the symbolic core of the Emerson clan: the house. In evaluating the development of houses and private space from an anthropological perspective, Peter J. Wilson states that "throughout the domesticated world the house . . . serves not simply as a dwelling, shelter, and spatial arrangement of activities but also as a central instrument through which people record and express their thoughts."[12] In the novel, Tyler's descriptions of the Emerson house reveal a similar view of its symbolic importance.

The opening paragraph of *The Clock Winder* lifts the curtain to reveal a house which, like Mrs. Emerson, has "outlived its usefulness" (*CW* 1) but still seems violated by the presence and action of Richard the handyman. Elizabeth's respect for the home is evident in her attitude toward its maintenance. While Mrs. Emerson would rather "set antique vases over the scars on the dining room buffet and [lay] more and more Persian carpets over the worn spots on the floors," (*CW* 29) Elizabeth wants to "sand the floors down to the bare grain" (*CW* 29). Unlike her children, who would argue that Mrs. Emerson is not getting old, Elizabeth readily accepts painful limitations: she admits that she can mend, carry firewood, and maintain tools, but "there's damage you can't repair" (*CW* 225).

What she *can* repair, however, is central to the operation of the home and the family. In a letter asking Elizabeth to return, Matthew clearly links the home with its occupants' emotional states:

> Without you we are falling apart. The basement has started seeping at the corners. Mother says she wouldn't even know what to look under in the yellow pages, for a job like that. Elizabeth should be here, she said. She knew the names of things. (*CW* 178)

In the intimate relationship Elizabeth develops with the house and the Emersons, she accepts her role as the necessary outsider. She considers the house and the family rundown. But with sympathy and nonchalance, she ambles through the garden with Mrs. Emerson; she calmly reassures her that the feelings of clumsiness after her stroke will pass; and "while Mrs. Emerson napped, Elizabeth wound all the clocks" (*CW* 269). Her initiation into the clan develops, in part, because of her connection to the home.

The joking and avoidance relationships described in kinship studies are another central feature of Elizabeth's developing connection with the Emersons. Fred Eggan, discussing the balance between respect, avoidance, and joking relationships, points out that many in-law relationships—sharing a home but not blood—make conflicts inevitable, and joking becomes "a social necessity for avoiding or minimizing conflict if the household organization is to function properly."[13] In addition to releasing emotional tensions, obligatory joking relationships "establish bonds between such relatives which gradually bind them together."[14] This special alliance has no specific duties except "not to take offense at the disrespect so long as it is kept within certain bounds defined by custom."[15]

Elizabeth Abbot allows herself to be discussed, lightly mocked, and teased. In the scene in which Elizabeth is supposed to prove herself by butchering a turkey, Elizabeth understands that she has no choice but to endure these taunting comments by Timothy: "Out walking your turkey, I see" (*CW* 41); "I could run over him with my car if you like" (*CW* 41). She is teased with labels such as "Miss Easy-Going" and "Miss Fix-It" (*CW* 64). Even Mrs. Emerson enjoys flaunting her "handyman" before her friends, and Elizabeth simply smiles and shuffles on. Andrew's avoidance of this intruder elicits a similar response. Elizabeth knows that Andrew has chosen to avoid her, and her only position is to respect and tolerate his wishes: "she kept an ear tuned for the sound of his approach, and circled rooms where he might be" (*CW* 264). The joking and avoidance relationships thus diffuse hostility toward the outsider and illustrate her position as the handyman of the clan.

The more formal process of Elizabeth's initiation resembles a primitive ritual of marking the initiate as a sign of acceptance. As in many cultures, the initiate chooses the moment when she is ready for the rights and responsibilities of the clan.[16] She allows Andrew to shoot her, and the flesh wound symbolizes both her accepting responsibility for Timothy's death and their accepting her into the clan. Andrew, who has hated Elizabeth to the point of death threats, immediately after shooting her treats her as kin, fussing over her and asking, "Did I hurt you?" (*CW* 280). The transformation in Elizabeth is even more profound. Just before the shooting, she directly refuses Matthew's marriage proposal, offering this explanation of her position in the family:

> "It's funny," she said. "*I* picture us with your family tangled up in everything you do, and me brought in to watch. Your mother living with us, and long distance phone calls from sisters divorcing and brothers having breakdowns, and quarrels among the lot of you every evening over the supper table. And me on the outside, wondering what next. Putting on the Band-Aids. Someone to impress." (*CW* 276–77)

Her reaction to being shot brings her to the inside of the circle: she is laughing, dismissing Andrew's attempted murder as a quirk. Dr. Felson accentuates the transformation by recognizing Elizabeth as an Emerson not only in her injury but in her bemused explanation about Andrew: "Oh, well, he's apologized" (*CW* 282). The inner circle of the Emerson family is appropriately presented in the closing of Chapter 12; they are all packed into Matthew's car, and Elizabeth opens "the door to pile in among a tangle of other Emersons" (*CW* 282). Elizabeth has transcended the label of Other to become an *other* Emerson.

The initiation is complete with a renaming of the former outsider. Elizabeth is thereafter called Gillespie, a jumbling caused by Mrs. Emerson's stroke. The initiation becomes an important part of their lore, as the family explains to P.J., the latest outsider: "You mustn't mind Andrew, J.C. He's hard on outsiders. The second time he met *Gillespie,* he shot her." (*CW* 300) To P.J., Gillespie is as bewildering as all the others, for she laughs gently with Andrew about the incident and stomps through the house on a locust-seeking mission. The question of whether this initiation is a triumph or defeat remains unresolved as the novel ends. If she wants to fit in with the Emersons, P.J. must endure the same trials and re-education that have transformed Elizabeth. As Tyler herself suggests in her comment that "Elizabeth does herself irreparable damage,"[17] the cost of this initiation is dear.

In all of her novels, Anne Tyler preserves and celebrates what is distinct about kinship—the rituals, codes, language, and myths that separate one group from another. Yet she offers no clear conclusion about the American family. Even the narrative pattern is often distressing. As Mary F. Robertson states, "because the boundary between insiders and outsiders is continually transgressed, the progress of Tyler's novels is felt more as an expansion of narrative disorder than as a movement toward resolution and clarification."[18] The tension between the distinct, ideal family and the pulls of the twentieth century also underlies Tyler's novels. Her contemporary settings reflect a growing cultural and intellectual homogeneity: we watch the same television programs, eat in identical restaurants coast to coast, play the same board games, listen to the same music, buy family vacation packages, rent the same videocassettes, reheat the same processed foods in our microwave ovens. Yet the conversations, private agonies, and rituals in Tyler's work remind us of the primitive ties that bind, the ways in which, even in a mobile society with few conventionally biogenetic families, we remain fortunately and tragically allied to our kin.

NOTES

1. David M. Schneider, "American Kinship: A Cultural Account" (1968), rpt. in *Readings in Kinship and Social Structure,* ed. Nelson Graburn (New York: Harper & Row, 1971), p. 393.

2. "Kinship" (1930), rpt. in *Readings in Kinship,* p. 102.

3. "Home at Last, and Homesick Again: The Ten Novels of Anne Tyler," *The Hollins Critic,* 23 (April 1986), 6.

4. (1949), trans. James Harle Bell and John Richard von Sturmer, ed. Rodney Needham (Boston: Beacon Press, 1969), pp. 478–85.

5. "The Fiction of Anne Tyler," *The Southern Quarterly,* 21 (4) (Summer 1983), 35.

6. "The Kith and the Kin," in *Character of Kinship,* ed. Jack Goody (London: Cambridge University Press, 1973), p. 94.

7. Clifford Geertz, *The Interpretation of Cultures: Selected Essays* (New York: Basic Books, 1973), pp. 353–54.

8. *A Critique of the Study of Kinship* (Ann Arbor: University of Michigan Press, 1984), p. 165.

9. Edward Hoagland, "About Maggie, Who Tried Too Hard," *The New York Times Book Review,* 11 September 1988, p. 43.

10. "Order and Disorder in Oral Tradition," in *Anthropology and Myth: Lectures 1951–1982* (1984), trans. Roy Willis (Oxford: Basil Blackwell, 1987), p. 123.

11. *Safe at Last in the Middle Years: The Invention of the Midlife Progress Novel: Saul Bellow, Margaret Drabble, Anne Tyler, and John Updike* (Berkeley: University of California Press, 1988), p. 111.

12. *The Domestication of the Human Species* (New Haven: Yale University Press, 1988), p. 66.

13. "Respect and Joking Relationships Among the Cheyenne and Arapaho" (1937), rpt. in *Readings in Kinship,* p. 142.

14. Ibid., p. 144.

15. A. R. Radcliffe-Brown, "On Joking Relationships" (1940), rpt. in *Readings in Kinship,* p. 149.

16. Robin Clarke and Geoffrey Hindley, *The Challenge of the Primitives* (New York: McGraw-Hill, 1975), pp. 107–08.

17. Clifford Ridley, "Anne Tyler: A Sense of Reticence Balanced by 'Oh Well, Why Not?'" [rev. of *The Clock Winder*], *National Observer,* 11 (July 1972), 23.

18. "Anne Tyler: Medusa Points and Contact Points," in *Contemporary American Women Writers: Narrative Strategies,* ed. Catherine Rainwater and William J. Scheick (Lexington: University Press of Kentucky, 1985), p. 122.

Mentors and Maternal Role Models: The Healthy Mean between Extremes in Anne Tyler's Fiction

THERESA KANOZA

The outrageously unconventional mother-in-law is a recurring character in Anne Tyler's novels. Typically a footloose eccentric and often a widow, she lives outside society's mainstream, and her existence does not depend on a man. This feisty, self-sufficient woman invariably opposes in manner and personality the female protagonist's own mother, and she usually enjoys the favor of her daughter-in-law. Charlotte Ames of *Earthly Possessions* longs for the eventful life of the wildly exuberant Alberta Emory, the mother of her future husband Saul. She delights in Alberta, a "gypsyish type, beautiful . . . carelessly dressed . . . surprisingly young" (*EP* 64) who abandons her husband to marry his father; she despairs at her own mother, the defeated Lacey Ames who suffocates under her obesity in a silent, dreary house. *Celestial Navigation*'s Mary Tell revels in the sleazy world she temporarily inhabits with her husband's mother Gloria, a "peroxide blonde forever in shorts and a halter" (*CN* 71). The brassy young widow, whose carefree life consists of watching television soap operas, reading confession magazines, and having an occasional drinking binge when her truck driver boyfriend passes through town, opens her home to Mary when she flees her sheltered youth and her religious, elderly parents. Elizabeth Abbott's mother in *The Clock Winder* (whose first name is never mentioned, appropriately so since she gleans her identity from her role as her husband's wife and her children's mother) hides her own strength to bolster her husband's ego. "From the day they're born till the day they die," she counsels Elizabeth, "men are being protected by women [but] if you breathe a word of this . . . I'll deny it" (*CW* 160). While Mrs. Abbott willingly limits her sphere of influence to the kitchen, the plucky Pamela Emerson, Elizabeth's future mother-in-law, has always held herself superior to her late husband and tries to maintain a firm hold on herself and her rapidly fleeing family. Marveling at the cantankerous grand dame's struggle to present an image of competence, composure, and class, Elizabeth exclaims with sincerity, "Think what a small life she has, but she still dresses up everyday and holds her stomach in. Isn't that something?" (*CW* 110)

The hero's adventurous, self-aware, often self-promoting mother-in-law balances the thoroughly domestic and ineffectual mother, and she sanctions by example her son's wife's desire for personal fulfillment. Jean Baker Miller explains in *Toward a New Psychology of Women* that women often languish in their subordinate status, refusing to test their strength by challenging gender norms and thus remain dependent on their husbands. Other women, contends Miller, disguise capability with deference and feigned passivity. Rather than openly acknowledging their own personal needs, they transform them into the needs of the men and children in their lives. By effectively serving others, they insure their place in their family's lives and downplay the power they wield in the home.[1] The traditional mothers of Tyler's protagonists include the helpless, emotional invalid and the self-effacing martyr of whom Miller speaks. Occupying the opposite end of the scale is the winsome but often narcissistic mother-in-law whose self-absorption frequently jeopardizes a stable home environment. Such diametrically opposed role models result in a hybrid, a young wife who blends the best qualities the older women possess without their extremes toward either the bizarre or the rigidly conventional. Tyler's protagonist seeks to become secure, savvy, and autonomous, while remaining firmly grounded in family life.

Elizabeth Abbott is first presented as a young woman destined to fail. For her parents, the aimless college drop-out pales when compared to their younger daughter Polly who has fulfilled their every expectation. The former high school May Day Queen, Polly pursued secretarial training, then settled down with a local boy to become a housewife and mother. Lady-like in appearance, she stands in stark contrast to the misfit Elizabeth, who opts for a uniform of blue jeans, white shirt, and moccasins. Mr. Abbott is eager but doubtful that his elder daughter will conform to the traditional feminine role, and he chastises her slovenly habits: "I never saw anyone live the way you do. Week after week you rise late and lie around the house all day, your appearance is disorderly . . . and your mother says you are no help at all . . . . You're disrupting an entire household." (*CW* 156) An added point of contention is Elizabeth's refusal to join the Baptist church, of which her father is pastor, and her avowed belief in reincarnation. Regarded as a black sheep for her nonconformity, Elizabeth fulfills her parents' prophecies of failure. She blunders through a series of jobs as proofreader, envelope stuffer, and letter carrier, and develops a pathological fear of influencing anyone for fear her effect will be disastrous. But in the unlikely position as handyman for the aging widow Pamela Emerson, Elizabeth's successes mount, and her self-esteem builds.

Elizabeth admires and in time emulates her employer's fortitude yet sees the fear which her brave spirit masks. Like the deteriorating house in which she raised her children, Mrs. Emerson has outlived her usefulness. Life on her own now is frightening, but, worthy of the surname which she shares with the American seer and advocate of self-reliance Ralph Waldo, she refuses to crumble as a widow. Through painstaking grooming she presents to the world a poised, if aging, matriarch: "When the children visited and she stood at the door to meet them, wearing pastels, holding out her smooth white hands with polished nails, she saw how relieved they looked . . . she had survived their desertion, she had not become a broken old lady after all" (*CW* 7).

Ironically, just as Pamela's grasp at self-sufficiency is a positive influence on Elizabeth, the widow's dependence on Elizabeth also nourishes the handyman's self-concept. Mrs. Emerson knows nothing of Elizabeth's past and thus frees the young woman from her history of failure to blossom into a competent caretaker in response to Pamela's demands: "From the day that Elizabeth first climbed those porch steps, a born fumbler and crasher and dropper of precious objects, she had possessed miraculous repairing powers, and Mrs. Emerson . . . had obligingly presented her with a faster and faster stream of disasters in need of attention" (*CW* 79).

Pamela's faith in Elizabeth is balm to her wounded ego. As Nancy Friday explains in *My Mother/My Self*, the alienation a daughter faces when she rejects her mother's lifestyle is compounded by guilt over disappointing her parents and feelings of inadequacy for not meeting their expectations. This separation from the parents, often painful but necessary if individuation is to occur, is facilitated by a female role model. "We have abilities, talents, the potential to go long distances," says Friday, "but until somebody sees us, recognizes our secret selves, we will go the short distance and remain the safe, unexplored person."[2] Nourished by Pamela's confidence, Elizabeth's "secret self" develops:

She awoke here every morning feeling amazed all over again that she had finally become a grownup. Where to go and when to sleep and what to do with the day were hers to decide—or not to decide, which was even better. She could leave here when she wanted or stay forever, fixing things. In this house everything she touched seemed to work out fine. Not like the old days. (*CW* 38)

But Elizabeth's road to autonomy is not without pitfalls. Whereas Pamela Emerson's demands on her handyman are backed by trust and allow Elizabeth to raise her low opinion of herself, the matriarch's overbearing manner alienates her own family. Elizabeth is cast as the buffer between mother and children, a frightening role for a woman who fears influence over another. When Timothy Emerson is expelled from medical school and also suspects losing Elizabeth to his brother Matthew, he commits suicide, killing Elizabeth's fledgling belief in herself as well. She blames herself for his death and resents the Emersons for pulling her into their morass of family problems. Shell-shocked, she retreats to her parents' home in North Carolina and works as a companion to the elderly Mr. Cunningham. She risks little of herself in this position since the infirm old man is expected to die soon.

The thrill of power Elizabeth felt as the competent handyman, however, lures her back to Baltimore to care for Mrs. Emerson after she suffers a stroke. Pamela is bedridden and partially paralyzed but as Elizabeth witnesses her determination to regain independence, the two women re-enter their former symbiosis, an affiliation which strengthens and defines their individual characters rather than dissolves or merges their identities.[3] Elizabeth is the clock winder, restoring life to Pamela Emerson. Under Elizabeth's care which is attentive but not smothering, Pamela recovers her health and her poise. Mrs. Emerson similarly renews Elizabeth, the believer in reincarnation. Elizabeth escapes fatal injury at the gun of paranoid Andrew Emerson, who blames her for his brother's death, but incurs a wound which she feels settles the score for Timothy's suicide. In this second chance at life, Mrs. Emerson christens her "Gillespie," the closest she can come with her impaired speech to pronouncing "Elizabeth." The new name solidifies Elizabeth's strong, assured identity: "The name Gillespie rang in her ears—the new person Mrs. Emerson was changing her into, [was] someone effective and managerial who was summoned by her last name, like a WAC" (*CW* 271). Pamela's faith strengthens Elizabeth's self-concept, and she teaches by example that while intrusion into the lives of others can wreak havoc, life without risking involvement, though safe, is barren.

The final scene presents the extended Emerson family: the married couple Elizabeth and Matthew and their two children, as well as Pamela and Andrew. As Elizabeth prepares the family dinner and breast-feeds her daughter, who "cling[s] like a barnacle" (*CW* 311), she seemingly re-enacts her mother's all-consuming domesticity. Lending to the possibility of marriage and family life as archetypal enclosure, a debilitating situation which Annis Pratt describes in *Archetypal Patterns in Women's Fiction,* is the

31

Emersons' quarantine at home as they seek shelter from the locust onslaught and look to Elizabeth to seal off the house.[4] But "Gillespie," as the androgynous name implies, is not the traditional housewife. Unlike Mrs. Abbott who masterfully runs her home from behind a mask of dependency and cunningly smooths away conflicts while asserting that her husband is the dominant caretaker, the capable Gillespie openly relishes her reputation as the unflappable "juggler of supplies, obtaining and distributing all her family needed" (*CW* 310). Despite images of enclosure, Gillespie enjoys what Pratt terms the rare marriage of equality, a union which liberates rather than limits her.[5]

Though she is clearly the family caretaker and her husband Matthew the breadwinner, the two transcend gender stereotypes to achieve a reciprocity which all the while preserves their individual identities. In his final appearance in the novel, sensitive Matthew is protective but also vulnerable. He is "stooped and skinny . . . . Gillespie, sheltered under his arm, smiled up at him and said, 'You look tired'" (*CW* 303). Their stance reflects the mutual support which two distinctively separate individuals provide when they come together. As Matthew's arm shelters Gillespie, her strong shoulder props him up. Wise Gillespie encourages Peter, the wandering Emerson who is her youngest brother-in-law, to treasure his new wife P.J.'s offbeat ways though his family sees her as a hopeless misfit. To his defeatist comment that "you shouldn't hope for anything from someone that much different from your family," Gillespie advises, "you should if your family doesn't have it" (*CW* 311). Obvious differences between her maternal role models have shaped Gillespie, uncovering new possibilities of being; she thus sees that differences between separate but equal mates should not necessarily be reconciled, or smoothed away, for they nourish and clarify the self.

Charlotte Ames' evolution in *Earthly Possessions* is also traceable to her mother-in-law, though Alberta Emory's inspiration is more subtle, less direct than Pamela Emerson's. Clearly, the vivacious Alberta is the antithesis of Lacey Ames, Charlotte's sullen mother, and she represents the full, breezy life Charlotte longs for. The indomitable Alberta's days brim with change and complication that delight rather than confound the free spirit. Charlotte withers in the jail that is her parents' house, "stale, dark, ancient . . . in which nothing had moved for a very long time" (*EP* 12), and craves news from Alberta's busy world. "Needless to say," recounts Charlotte, "I loved her. I hung on everything she told me . . . . I wished she would adopt me. I longed for her teeming house and riches . . . [and] eventfulness." (*EP* 64) Compared to Alberta, her own mother represents a deathly stasis. A sad, obese woman prone to breaking the furniture she sits on, she passes her days eating chocolate caramels, crocheting pincushions, and worrying that her husband or daughter will desert her.

Charlotte's connection to Alberta is short-lived. She is still a schoolgirl when Alberta runs off with her own father-in-law, a move that inspires in the adolescent the glamour of impetuous flight.[6] Charlotte remains, however, saddled with her mother well into adulthood. When a heart attack kills her father, Charlotte is forced to relinquish her freedom—a math scholarship to Markson College—to return home to Clarion to care for her helpless mother. Marriage to Alberta's son Saul, a boarder in the Ames' house, looms as her next chance to escape from home. But after marrying Charlotte and remaining in her mother's house, Saul becomes the town minister—his attempt to find the purpose and meaning missing from his early life with the reckless Alberta—and further chains his wife to the home of her youth. Charlotte plots her escape but becomes the silently begrudging caretaker not only of her husband, their daughter, and her mother who is slowly dying of cancer, but also of a ragtag assortment of waifs from the Holy Basis Church and of Saul's confused brothers who return home in their own search of stability.

Charlotte's relatively brief contact with Alberta allows her a glimpse of a woman with a seemingly firm sense of herself—a quality her own mother lacks. Lacey Ames manifests the problems which Nancy Chodorow in "Family Structure and Feminine Personality" reveals typically beset a Western, middle class woman in her struggle for individuation. If a woman grows up without establishing adequate ego boundaries, predominantly defining herself as someone's daughter, wife, or mother, she develops a poor self-image and later discourages the breaking of her daughter's dependence. The daughter inherits the legacy of low self-esteem and likewise defines herself relationally, perpetuating an unhealthy hold on her daughter, whose dependence affirms her own existence.[7] Thus, Lacey's ego boundary confusion becomes a stumbling block in Charlotte's own quest for autonomy.

Lacey married and reared a child in the same house that she grew up in, the same house in which Charlotte raises her family. Neither woman leaves home; both give birth to an only daughter. Lacey's happiest memories are of pleasing her widower father, acting as hostess at his dinner parties. After his death, her life stands still until she marries the traveling photographer Murray Ames. But seeing herself as indistinguishable from her husband, she blames him for her narrow existence: "Her husband just never had learned to fit in . . . . He wasn't outgoing enough. He acted so glum . . . . No wonder their life had shrunk and dwindled so." (*EP* 11) Alberta is proof, on the other hand, that even a married woman can take control of her own life. "But what about Alberta?" Charlotte questions. "Her husband was no good whatsoever, and still she had more friends than I could count" (*EP* 12).

Alberta also aids in the development of Charlotte's healthy sexual identity. Nancy Friday explains that a mother often discourages a daughter's emergent sexuality because it arouses the shame and disgust she felt about her own body, and she fears that her daughter's sexual identity is added impetus to separate from her. In cases where motherhood signals the end of a woman's expressed sexuality, a daughter requires an outside role model still in touch with her own physical desires to help her accept her blossoming sexuality.[8] Earthy, slouchy, often barefoot, Alberta exudes a relaxed sexuality, a drive that her elopement late in life attests to. Her lush sensuality balances Lacey's sexual austerity. Charlotte notes her parents' bed, "the middle of [which] stayed perfectly neat—a median strip unrumpled, undisturbed" (*EP* 12) and the mystery of her own conception. "I can't imagine how it happened," explains her mother, "we hardly ever did much" (*EP* 181). But Alberta's expression of her own libido sanctions Charlotte's sex drive. Before her wedding she moves into Saul's bedroom, lured by his "salty and wild" scent that will arouse her throughout her married life. As she braves her mother's scorn to slip into his bed, Charlotte sees Alberta's house basked in moonlight and framed by the bedroom window.

As Nancy Chodorow explains, a daughter whose mother's ego is not well-defined inherits more than a poor self-concept. Lacking a sense of herself as an autonomous entity, she does not differentiate herself from the rest of the world and bears an unlocalized sense of responsibility for the actions and well-being of others.[9] Like her own mother, Charlotte finds it difficult to claim herself. She runs her father's photography studio for seventeen years, longer than he runs it himself, but persists in seeing it only as a temporary position. She is a daughter, wife, and mother; an actual livelihood bears no legitimacy for her. Jake Simms, Charlotte's bank robber captor, uncannily sums up the weakness the two restive travelers share: "Any time you see someone running, it's their old, faulty self they're running from. Or other people's notion of their faulty self." (*EP* 157)

Charlotte is locked in her poor self-concept by what she misconstrues as another's low opinion of her. Her accomplishments, coveted hallmarks of a teenager's success—cheerleading, honor societies, her title as most vivacious and best groomed girl in the senior class—mean little to her. She is trapped in her own dark reality: "I knew the picture we made: fat mother in elastic stockings, shriveled father, sullen spinster daughter" (*EP* 58). She later repudiates Saul's love for her, insisting that he harbors a secret grudge against her for her lack of religious faith. Jake points out Charlotte's self-deprecating solipsism which forces her to discredit any praise. "Maybe . . . you just had him figured wrong to start with. I mean," explains Jake, "it could be he really does believe you're good, and worries what that means for his side. Ever thought of that?" (*EP* 164) Such a self-affirming concept is foreign to Charlotte. Similarly, when her brother-in-law Amos marvels at her dedication and strengths as she nurses her dying mother and cares for the sundry members of the Emory household, Charlotte is convinced he misreads her yet hopes he will retain his flattering but incorrect image of her.

The photographs her father takes of her as a child, the bank's video tape of Jake taking her hostage, and the gas station restroom mirrors she looks into as she and Jake make their way south afford Charlotte ample opportunity to view her own image, but the person she sees is always a stranger. Having planned to run away with Saul's brother Amos, a romantic flight that would parallel Alberta's own departure, she cannot recognize herself as the attractive woman her brother-in-law perceives. Gliding past a mirror she remarks, "I was accompanied by someone beautiful: her hair filled with lights, eyes deep with plots, gypsyish dress a splash of color in the dusk" (*EP* 176). She accepts as her due the disapproval she mistakenly believes people feel for her, and she rejects their endorsement. Still failing to realize that a personality is protean, comprised of facets that develop through expression, Charlotte holds too tightly to her father's defeatism. "I never have held with these fancied-up photographs," he tells Charlotte of her own whimsical work. "No sense pretending someone is what he isn't" (*EP* 58).

But Alberta is the agent who indirectly moves her to a broader vision. Looking back on that schoolgirl infatuation with her, Charlotte realizes that despair may have prompted Alberta Emory to desert her family: "I was easily fooled by appearances. Maybe all families, even the most normal-looking, were as queer as ours once you got up close to them. Maybe Alberta was secretly as sad as my mother." (*EP* 65) Lacey's explanation that insecurity drove Alberta to enhance her image through scandal rings true when Charlotte considers that "people are only reflections in other people's eyes" (*EP* 141). This awareness is exhilarating rather than disenchanting, freeing Charlotte from her self-condemning solipsism. She can accept the Emorys' description of their mother as "pushy, clamorous, violent, taking over their lives, meddling in their brains, demanding a constant torrent of admiration and gaiety" (*EP* 150) without relinquishing her uplifting version of Alberta.

Likewise, Charlotte reconciles herself within the framework of her memories. Questioning the veracity of her childhood recollections, she doubts that her mother was as unhappy as she thought, wonders if Lacey was even fat, and accepts that her memory of being a changeling was her own fancy. She realizes that though one is not defined by another's perceptions, emerging qualities can be reinforced by another's reading of them. Showy Alberta's acting out, therefore, was her attempt to free up what was locked inside. Always certain that people saw her weaknesses, Charlotte begins to trust her strengths and to know that others recognize them as well. The road to adventure leads Charlotte back to herself and her family, eager to explore the wealth of variety and riches which they provide. Home from her long-awaited journey and at-home with her life, the enlightened Charlotte realizes the power of her "fancied up" photographs of subjects masquerading in Alberta's cast-off costumes. "I've come to believe," she muses, "that their borrowed medals may tell more truths than they hide" (*EP* 200).

In *Celestial Navigation,* unlike *The Clock Winder* and *Earthly Possessions,* where women enjoy personal emancipation within the bonds of marriage, Mary Tell's quest for autonomy—charted in essence by her mother-in-law who is a minor character with tremendous impact—will not accommodate a husband. Young Mary Darcy loves her cautious, devoted parents, but in the heat of her sexual awakening she fears nothing more than a destiny to relive their dull and narrow existence. Her elopement with reckless Guy Tell provides excitement, but tender Mary, who is pregnant and still a teenager, requires more security than her young husband can provide. The solution is Guy's mother. Gloria's slummy life—days full of shopping, television, and sleazy romance novels—satisfies Mary as her respectable girlhood never could. And yet Gloria has substance; she props up the new mother, as Mary's testimony reveals:

> I'm ashamed to say how much I leaned on her. She didn't interfere, she never tried to take over, but whenever I was feeling lost and too young she was right there handing me hot milk and talking on and on in that airy, fake-tough way she had, appearing not to notice anything was wrong but soothing all the same. Could a man do that? No man that I know of. (*CN* 72)

Gloria's grit engenders Mary's notion of female supremacy. Impressionable Mary reads into Gloria's strong capabilities that women are forced to become fearless survivors; men are a pleasant diversion but unreliable and expendable. Though Mary leaves Guy, she takes with her an image of the self-reliant Gloria, a widow whose happy routine includes men but does not depend on them. Like Charlotte Emory's connection with Alberta, Mary's time with Gloria is brief. As Nancy Friday stresses, however, young women do not need an ongoing relationship with their role model so much as an image of them to maintain, as both Charlotte and Mary have.[10]

After Mary deserts her husband Guy and moves into a Baltimore boarding house to be near her married lover John Harris, she is totally dependent on him. But although friendless, unemployed, and bound to her young daughter Darcy, she vows that even if she remarries she will earn money for the likely event that she will be out on her own again. Inherent in her pledge is the belief that men are unsteady. After John abandons her, Mary falls into a convenient common-law marriage to the agoraphobic artist and boarding house proprietor Jeremy Pauling. The set-up represents her reliance on yet another man, but she never gives up her struggle for autonomy.

Mary seemingly forgets her youth with her reserved, industrious parents, but often recalls her lazy days with Gloria. She eventually sends her mother-in-law a birthday card, establishing a connection through which Guy later relays news of their finalized divorce. Sensing Gloria's disapproval of her desertion of Guy and imagining her disappointment at her subsequent dependence on a series of men, Mary taps into unknown reserves of strength to stabilize her life with the ineffectual Jeremy. She flourishes in her role as housewife and mother, giving birth to five children with Jeremy and meeting life's demands head-on. As he observes the great stores of provisions she stockpiles for their family and for the larger clan of boarders, Jeremy perceives her as "supplier, feeder, caretaker. 'See how I give?'" he imagines Mary asks. "'And how I keep on giving . . . . I will always have more, you don't even have to ask. I will be waiting with a new shirt for you the minute the elbows wear through in the old one.'" (*CN* 160)

Her constant vigilance which anticipates her family's every need is reminiscent of Gloria's care for her. But whereas a frightened teenaged mother would be reassured by such a safety net, it is demeaning to a middle-aged father of five—even if his incompetence requires such a back-up. Mary's strength does not allow Jeremy to overcome his own weakness. Her decision to spare him the trauma of the hospital trip when their son is born underscores her lack of faith in his capability, despite his previous successful visits to the maternity ward. Her verve drains Jeremy; her strong bearing erases him. When she enters the studio which is his domain, he notes that "the room appeared to be hers . . . . When she stepped back to look at the statue, he had the feeling that was hers too." (*CN* 177) He can only dream that she needs him, that she will call upon him for comfort. Eager to become a participating member of the family, he reads up on fatherhood only to learn that "none of that advice [came] in handy. Mary made her own nest." (*CN* 172)

Jeremy withdraws from Mary, a retreat to bind up his tattered ego. He seals himself off in his studio, forgetting their wedding day which would formalize their common-law marriage. Hurt and confused by his distance, Mary perceives it as his wish to be free of family entanglements. Her earlier prophecy that another man would cast her off has come true, and she makes good on her previous resolution. Financed by her meager savings from money-back offers and pay-offs from household hints, she moves her family into the boathouse shack which she rents from Brian, Jeremy's agent. The surroundings are bleak, but Mary finds work in a day-care center and settles her children in to stay. When Jeremy braves bus schedules and unfamiliar landmarks to locate her, he finds her well-adjusted. "I'm managing on my own now," she explains, both out of pride in her accomplishment and to mask the pain of his rejection. "I'm not depending on a soul. I'm doing it on my own." (*CN* 266)

Jeremy hopes to match her competence by assuming her duty of rowing the children out to Brian's boat to air the sails. Though Mary recognizes his need to prove himself and realizes that she has always overwhelmed him with her power and energy, she cannot risk her children's safety. Her lack of faith, however warranted, destroys him. He retreats to his Baltimore studio, never to venture out again unassisted. Mary arrives at the self-sufficiency she witnessed in Gloria, her life with Jeremy the training ground for such autonomy: "I learned my lesson the first time around. Women should never leave any vacant spots for the men to fill; they should form an unbroken circle on their own and enclose each child within it." (CN 197)

Mary's solitariness seems a severe, self-imposed exile, but it can be seen as a stage in her development. Charlotte Emory and Elizabeth Emerson find personal fulfillment within their roles as wives, but they have relatively well-adjusted husbands who come to appreciate their spouses' autonomy and who also participate in parenting. Fragile Jeremy cannot effectively share family responsibilities nor fathom his wife's needs, hence Mary's overcompensating strength which further stifles his timid attempts to contribute to his home life. Yet if Mary were once secure in her hard-won self-sufficiency, she would presumably feel free enough to open her life to men, just as her mentor mother-in-law chose to do.

Tyler's last two novels reveal variations on the theme of the protagonist's liberation which results from her connections with her unconventional mother-in-law. Upon her husband's death in *The Accidental Tourist,* flashy Alicia Leary packs her children off to their grandparents' home in Baltimore and sets out to explore the world. When her staid sons marry, she consoles their wives for the lackluster lives they have entered. The marked affinity between Alicia and Muriel Pritchett, Alicia's son's lively girlfriend who revitalizes the grieving Macon, includes their freewheeling behavior as well as their gaudy appearance. *Breathing Lessons*'s Maggie Moran, influenced herself by her friend Serena's unwed, barmaid mother Anita, resuscitates her stifled family with her zany unpredictability. She shamelessly interferes in her children's lives but rekindles domestic warmth within her fragmented family as she charges ahead. Her daughter-in-law Fiona's maternal instincts only flicker, but under the tutelage of Maggie—Fiona's confidant and former labor coach—the young woman leaves her dour mother and attempts to reunite her own estranged immediate family. Through contact with a strong mother-in-law, Tyler's heroes move toward the personal fulfillment their own mothers lack. The hero becomes neither her eccentric, often self-absorbed mother-in-law nor her own passive, self-sacrificing mother. Extracting the best of both role models she becomes her own person, able to nurture herself as well as her family.

NOTES

1. (Boston: Beacon Press, 1976), pp. 10–14.
2. *My Mother/My Self: The Daughter's Search for Identity* (New York: Delecorte Press, 1977), p. 201.

3. Women need not sacrifice affiliations to attain individuation, as men often do. Women quite validly seek something more complete than autonomy as it is defined for men, a fuller not a lesser ability to encompass relationships to others, simultaneous with the fullest development of the self. Women do not need to set affiliation and strength in opposition one against the other. They can readily integrate the two and search for more and better ways to use affiliation to enhance strength, and strength to enhance affiliation. Miller, *Toward a New Psychology of Women* (n. 1), pp. 95–96.

4. (Bloomington: Indiana University Press, 1981), p. 48.

5. Ibid., p. 57.

6. While a girl typically finds a role model in early childhood, she is also open to such influence throughout adolescence and into her twenties as Tyler's impressionable protagonists prove to be. *My Mother/My Self,* p. 202.

7. In *Women, Culture, and Society,* ed. Michelle Zimbalist Rosaldo and Louise Lamphere (Stanford University Press, 1974), pp. 55–66.

8. *My Mother/My Self,* p. 201.

9. *Woman, Culture, and Society,* p. 58.

10. *My Mother/My Self,* p. 201.

Anne Tyler's Houses

Frank W. Shelton

In their very influential *The Madwoman in the Attic,* Sandra Gilbert and Susan Gubar discuss the role of houses and domestic space in the work of nineteenth-century women writers. They observe that "anxieties about space sometimes seem to dominate the literature of both nineteenth-century women and their twentieth-century descendants."[1] They posit a uniquely female tradition of the period: the dramatization of imprisonment and escape, with houses and domestic furnishings functioning as "primary symbols of female imprisonment."[2] In *The Madwoman in the Attic* and their succeeding volumes, Gilbert and Gubar write with a particularly feminist perspective; Anne Tyler, on the other hand, has few if any feminist intentions. In fact, in a review of Ellen Moers' *Literary Women,* one of the earlier treatments of the feminist tradition in literature, Tyler commented, "Only a portion of my life—and almost none of my writing life—is much affected by what sex I happen to be."[3] Yet all her novels center in one way or another on domestic life, and often she uses the very images of domestic entrapment and enclosure Gilbert and Gubar and others see as elements of a particularly female literary tradition. At least two things are different between Tyler and writers who fit more comfortably in the tradition. One is that she does not concentrate exclusively on women as protagonists; domestic life in her fiction can be just as frustrating for men as for women. Secondly, she does not portray freedom from the domestic as necessarily the desired goal, as other women writers sometimes do.

A consideration of houses and other images of domesticity in Tyler's works should begin with *Earthly Possessions,* which for the purposes of this discussion can be seen as her revisionist treatment of the tradition Gilbert

40

and Gubar have described. Charlotte Emery views the house in which she was raised and continues to live with her husband as a prison. The house is dark, drab and filled with useless objects. Charlotte sees her husband Saul as obsessive in his collection of more and more furniture. In her ironic way Charlotte describes the house and her husband: It "was overstuffed as it was, so he had to double things up: an end table in front of another end table, a sofa backed against the first. It was crazy. Every piece of furniture had its shadow, a Siamese twin." (*EP* 100–101) In addition to the furnishings, Saul collects people, bringing his brothers and other drifters home to stay with them. Charlotte is suffocated by such domestic arrangements. Her life principle is the opposite of her husband's: "My life has been a history of casting off encumbrances, paring down to the bare essentials, stripping for the journey. Possessions make me anxious." (*EP* 37) Ultimately Charlotte decides to flee all domestic encumbrances, but Tyler's ironic version of this tradition has her, after she flees, entrapped in a car. Particularly to Americans, the automobile is an image of mobility and of life stripped to the essentials, but, kidnapped by Jake Sims, Charlotte is no freer than she was. And when they pick up Mindy, Charlotte realizes that she cannot escape the competing demands of domestic life. She comes to discover that the dream of freedom is an illusion, that In fact she is more connected to the domestic than she thought. Near the end of the novel she looks at her neighborhood: "At the crumbling buildings across the street: the Thrift shop, newsstand, liquor store, Pei Wing the tailor . . . not a single home in the lot, come to think of it. Everyone else had moved on, and left us stranded here between the Amoco and the Texaco." (*EP* 185) One lone, almost pathetic family residence is left, and it is the site of domestic tension. Charlotte decides, however, that she must return. Thus Tyler acknowledges the entrapments of domesticity and the individual's desire to flee, but in her version of the female tradition she envisions the house as the setting of life as it must be lived.

Earthly Possessions clearly, perhaps too clearly and dialectically to be a major Tyler novel, delineates the tension in her fiction between inhabiting and emerging. Houses are related to inhabiting and shelter but may be a burden on individuals which they must shed, or attempt to shed, to become a whole being. In fact houses often embody the nature of the people living in them and the lives lived in them.

The first two novels of Tyler's maturity, *The Clock Winder* and *Celestial Navigation,* both focus on old, rundown houses. Though the Emerson house is located in Roland Park, a moneyed, upper-class section, both are gloomy and suggest the insularity of the lives lived within them. Mrs. Emerson spends a great deal of energy trying to keep up respectable appearances, but her house betrays her. "The house had outlived its usefulness. It sat hooded and silent, a brown shingleboard monstrosity . . ." (*CW* 3). It is stuffed with furniture and expensive antiques, but, far from providing comfort, the house is oppressive, especially to the younger Emersons. The Pauling house, located in the middle of the city, reflects the decaying inner city of Baltimore, and the fact that it is a boarding house mirrors the impermanence and fragmentation of city life. The two novels have similar plots: a woman of youth and vitality comes into the house and brightens it with her presence. Elizabeth Abbot, the handyman who repairs not only what is wrong with the house but also ultimately what is wrong with the family, marries Matthew Emerson and permanently infuses the Emerson family with some of her vitality. Mary Tell's similar effect on the Pauling household is more temporary. She ends up leaving Jeremy and the Pauling house and moving with her children to a rundown cabin on the Chesapeake Bay. *Celestial Navigation* is the first instance in Tyler's works of the significant use of contrasting houses. The cabin is a more precarious residence than the house, but its nearness to the water suggests a freedom and expansiveness which life in the Pauling house denies. Unlike Mrs. Emerson, Jeremy cannot be rescued from the backwater of his life and is left entombed in his decaying house.

Tyler's next novel, *Searching for Caleb*, emphasizes more consistently and more centrally different kinds of residences. Tyler clearly has a good deal of fun describing the Peck family houses in Roland Park. She explores the background of the Peck family in more detail than the Emersons; the first Peck to make money chose to build in Roland Park because of the respectability of the neighborhood, and he requires all his children to live in houses right next to him. The area is described as "staid chilly Roland Park with its damp trees and gloomy houses" (*SC* 148). Like other Tyler houses, these are stuffed with furniture and household decorations and crowded with people. The residences are oppressive to the younger Duncan and Justine. Duncan asserts with relish that the Peck houses remind him of "Hamsters. Or baby mice, or gerbils. Any of those little animals that cluster in one corner piled on top of each other even when they have a great big cage they are free to spread out in." (*SC* 81) With their identical houses, identical V-8 Fords and determination to shut out the world and associate only with other Pecks, the family is devoted to habit, routine, conformity.

Opposed to the Pecks in both lifestyle and choice of residence are Duncan and Justine. They move once a year to more and more precarious and shabby rental houses. When they first got married, they possessed a great many household furnishings, most of them gifts from the Pecks. But as they moved from year to year, Justine left more and more of their possessions behind, until at the time of present action in the novel they travel very light indeed. In reaction to the deadening habit and routine of their Peck family, they embrace movement, change, surprise and the unpredictable. Yet as the novel progresses, the reader gradually realizes that while this way of life seems to satisfy Duncan completely, Justine is less than fulfilled. Especially after her daughter marries, her grandfather dies, and Uncle Caleb leaves, Justine feels that in the impermanence of her life she has mislaid her self. Always enjoying their periodic visits to the Pecks more than Duncan does, near the end of the novel she seriously considers moving back to them, an action which would devastate Duncan. But Justine concocts an ingenious compromise. Rather than return to the Pecks, or go on as they have, they join a carnival, he as a fix-it man and she as fortune teller. They will live in a trailer, the most impermanent kind of residence yet in Tyler's fiction. But they will be members of the community of the carnival, and their movement will have some direction. Furthermore the carnival sets up in small Maryland towns, so in their movements they will continue to circle Baltimore. Thus Justine will have access to her family while at the same time retaining the independence and mobility which is so important to her and Duncan.

Morgan's Passing also makes use of two different residences, the house of Morgan and Bonny Gower and the apartment of Leon and Emily Meredith. The contrast repeats some of the elements of *Searching for Caleb,* but with a difference. The Gower house is a large, well-kept brick colonial. Yet Morgan hates it because of its *dis*order. While in its respectability the Peck house was the epitome of order, Morgan sees the opposite characteristics in his residence.

> Fool house! Something had gone wrong with it, somehow. It was so large and formal and gracious . . . . but underneath, Morgan never lost the feeling that something here was slipping. If they could just clear it out and start over, he sometimes thought. Or sell it! Sell it and have done with it, buy a plainer, more straightforward place. (*MP* 28–29)

He is especially oppressed by the clutter of both people and household furnishings. His advice is the Thoreauvian "simplify," discard everything not necessary. This chaotic house then embodies anything but the deadly dull routine of the Pecks. In search of a more orderly existence, Morgan fixes on the Merediths. They live in a sparsely furnished apartment in the center of the city, and Morgan likes to think they lead carefree, unattached lives with few possessions, just the kind of life he wants to live. But while it is true that their lives are simpler than the Gowers, they are not the itinerants he romanticizes them to be. In fact, when Emily visits the Gower house, she is charmed by all the activity and clutter she encounters.

One of the ironies of *Morgan's Passing* is that while Morgan and Emily are attracted to one another, they never fully gain mutual understanding. For example, when Morgan moves into Emily's apartment, Bonny in a fit of anger and revenge sends after him many of their household furnishings, as well as his mother and sister, and the apartment becomes filled to overflowing. It drives Morgan wild—he wants to leave it all and find a bare farm cabin. However,"Emily loved it all. She began to understand why Morgan's daughters kept coming home when they had to convalesce from something. You could draw vitality from mere objects, evidently. . . ." (*MP* 270) Morgan romanticizes Emily, feeling that she never becomes encumbered by material objects the way he does; the irony is that she wants to. *Morgan's Passing* concludes in a way similar to *Searching for Caleb*. Morgan and Emily reside in a trailer and are employed by the itinerant Holy Word Entertainment Troupe. Yet the ending of this novel does not seem the vital, positive compromise which concluded *Searching for Caleb*. Here Tyler actually takes the reader inside the trailer, and while Morgan has gotten his wish to live a more stripped down life, the trailer is drab and cramped. Morgan's vitality is not dimmed—the concluding sentence in the book is, "Everything he looked at seemed luminous and beautiful, and rich with possibilities" (*MP* 311). Yet the novel suggests that Morgan's dream of liberation and of a more orderly existence is an illusion, that human attachments and the disorder they bring with them are the conditions of existence. While life in the trailer is cramped and drab, however, Emily and Morgan clearly do continue to love one another.

To indicate how Tyler in various novels takes different perspectives on a similar situation, one need only compare *Morgan's Passing* and *The Accidental Tourist*. Morgan Gower is an eccentric who dreams of a more orderly life; Macon Leary, on the other hand, is an obsessively orderly man who by the end of the novel chooses a less structured, more extravagant existence. The Leary house is described early in the novel: "The house itself was medium-sized, unexceptional to look at, standing on a street of such houses in an older part of Baltimore. Heavy oak trees hung over it, shading it from the hot summer sun but also blocking breezes." (*AT* 9) Though Tyler spends little time on the details of this house, one can see that it is respectable, protected (and protecting), and suffocating. It is the seat of Macon's regular and very orderly life. After Sarah leaves, Macon allows absolutely no clutter in the house at all. This type of house embodies regularity, respectability, peace and safety, all the values which the Leary family, like the Pecks, holds dear.

At the opposite end of the spectrum are the houses and neighborhood of Muriel Pritchett. "Driving through the labyrinth of littered, cracked, dark streets in the south of the city, Macon wondered how Muriel could feel safe living here. There were too many murky alleys and stairwells full of rubbish and doorways lined with tattered shreds of posters." (*AT* 198) Her house is in a block of row houses "that gave a sense of having been skimped on. The roofs were flat, the windows flush and lacking depth. There was nothing to spare, no excess material for overhangs or decorative moldings, no generosity." (*AT* 199) Inside Muriel's house is all the chaos and clutter which Macon had so carefully excluded from his own life. Though he initially feels that this neighborhood is a foreign country, Macon gradually comes to appreciate the vitality of the place and the people who live there. He has a vision of his life in this place as "rich and full and astonishing" (*AT* 285). Of course, he continues his own habit of attempting to bring order to the world by making an effort to clean up the clutter of Muriel's house and fixing some of the things that need mending. But what is significant is that he finally chooses her house and her way of life—more messy, but also more vital and spontaneous and open to possibility—over his old house and old way of life—more regular and more peaceful but more muffled and closed off from possibility.

Yet an interesting feature of *The Accidental Tourist* is that a pair of minor characters move in the opposite direction. Macon's editor, Julian Edge, grown tired of life in a singles apartment building and realizing the emptiness of such a life, is attracted to and marries the obsessively orderly Rose Leary. When Rose cannot adapt to life in an apartment of their own, Julian moves back with her to the Leary house. Dissatisfied with the freedom and seemingly unlimited possibilities of single life, he desires the regularity and routine of a stable household. For Macon, the opposite is true; routine has become deadly, and he needs the richness of possibility Muriel offers him.

In her recent study of the midlife novel, Margaret Morganroth Gullette has observed that Tyler's "narratives of adulthood are packed with *things*—well packed, with each item in a fictionally useful place, crammed with meaning."[4] Houses and the domestic furnishings within them are important manifestations of such things. In Tyler's fiction houses function in the largest sense as physical and spiritual correlatives of people, for the space an individual chooses or is forced to inhabit in a meaningful way defines that individual. Imagery of spatial enclosure and escape is characteristic of the dialectic around which her work revolves, but it is difficult to derive a consistent stance from her novels, except to say that the dream of escape from entanglements is always illusory. The domestic arrangements of the individual characters, however, vary tremendously. Perhaps her central observation is contained in Macon Leary's insight at the conclusion of *The Accidental Tourist*. As he races toward a reunion with Muriel, "The real adventure, he thought, is the flow of time; it's as much adventure as anyone could wish" (*AT* 354). The flow of time involves change, openness to life. The large, old, respectable houses in Tyler's fiction usually suggest retreat from life and a smothering of the individual; however those houses can be revivified as they are in *The Clock Winder* and *Earthly Possessions*. On the other hand, a more impermanent kind of life in a less respectable residence like the trailers in *Searching for Caleb* and *Morgan's Passing* or Muriel's house in *The Accidental Tourist* can bring with it a receptivity to the vicissitudes of existence. Describing years ago why she writes, Tyler said, "I write because I want more than one life; I insist on a wider selection."[5]

Often trapped in unsatisfying domestic situations, her characters must at least be open to other perspectives and other modes of living. That often means trying out, either temporarily or permanently, a different kind of life at a different kind of residence. Her characters who are most successful in their own lives are those whose domestic arrangements combine, in whatever fashion they find that works for them, the opposing human needs for permanence and mobility.

NOTES

1. (New Haven: Yale University Press, 1979), p. 83.
2. Ibid., p. 85.
3. "Women Writers: Equal but Separate" [rev. of *Literary Women: The Great Writers*], *National Observer,* 15 (10 April 1976), 21.
4. *Safe at Last in the Middle Years: The Invention of the Midlife Progress Novel: Saul Bellow, Margaret Drabble, Anne Tyler, and John Updike* (Berkeley: University of California Press, 1988), p. 105.
5. "Because I Want More than One Life," *Washington Post,* 15 August 1976, sec. G, p. 7.

Art's Internal Necessity: Anne Tyler's *Celestial Navigation*

BARBARA HARRELL CARSON

In her essay "Still Just Writing," Anne Tyler speaks of the tension between creativity and life. How can the artist engage in the normal relationships of spouse and parent—relationships which unquestionably enrich one's art—without burying creativity under the everydayness of plastering the dining room ceiling; putting in time at the vet's and the kids' gym classes; and caring for sick children, dogs, and visiting uncles from Iran? Her own solution, Tyler says, has been to partition her life, walling off the creative from the domestic (at least as far as action is concerned)—forcing herself not to carry around the tape recorder while vacuuming, not letting herself sink back into a creative reverie when a child is sick. She has chosen, instead, to alternate regularly between the two separated worlds, confident that eventually the lived reality will enrich the artistic creation. (Speaking of her children, she writes: "They may have slowed down my writing for a while, but when I did write, I had more of a self to speak from.")[1] Jeremy Pauling in Tyler's novel *Celestial Navigation* faces a similar need to address the conflict between life and art, but he cannot achieve the accommodation that Tyler describes as her own.

Through Jeremy, Tyler explores the irony that lies so near the heart of creativity: deriving its energy from life, art comes to demand isolation from life in order to complete itself. Jeremy is initially driven to his art by a compulsion to a psychic wholeness that life has not afforded him, a need, we suspect, for something external to himself or for an external expression of his emotional state. Then, when his art no longer substitutes satisfactorily

47

for a real connection with the experiential world, Jeremy is compelled to search for completion in human relationships. The emotional wholeness found there causes his art to spiral to new heights (he too has more of self to speak from, then), but it also drives Jeremy to a new level of dissatisfaction. Now he is hounded by a need to retreat from lived reality in order to express artistically the vision his more complex life has given him. Tyler seems to be suggesting that for artists such as Jeremy the shadow side of the creation of art is destruction of human relationships, the rejection of the very thing art celebrates and clarifies. And for such artists, this destruction is not just the opposite of creativity, but the necessary ground out of which their art arises.

Thus, art and life become both allies and enemies. In trying to satisfy the now cooperating, now competing needs of both, the artist is driven by forces that make his life seem the working out of principles of necessity as inevitable as those in classical tragedy. We can imagine Tyler smiling benignly at declarations that "there is no 'must' in art, because art is always free."[2] While acknowledging the internal necessity of art that theorists like to talk about (the demand for aesthetic unity coming from the work of art itself), Tyler focuses on another kind of aesthetic determinism—the tangled forces of causality resident both in the artist's psyche and in the artistic process itself.

In the artist, the primary compulsion seems to be the urge to psychic balance, a need made particularly acute in Jeremy because of the psychic disequilibrium engendered by his mother. (Here, indeed, may be the source of the different solutions to the conflict between life and art arrived at by artists like Tyler and those like Jeremy.) A person with a secure sense of the distinction between self and other can be at ease with occasionally allowing the barriers between the two realms to blur (such as in moments of ecstasy brought on by mystical apprehension or by love or by creative fervor). As Frank Barron has pointed out, at such times "the strong self realizes that it can afford to allow regression [to a "primitive" state of union with other], because it is secure in the knowledge that it can correct itself."[3] Lacking such a strong self, Jeremy has made almost inpenetrable the walls between his psychic reality and the external world. It is his desperate attempt to shore up the self denied him by his mother. And art becomes almost the only point of contact between the two worlds.

But for Jeremy Pauling, art is a schizophrenogenic mother as surely as Mrs. Pauling was, giving him the same type of double-bind messages. Just as his mother repeatedly assured him of her love, while at the same time telling him how he had disappointed her, so life tells him to create *and* to love. But love, he comes to feel, limits his creativity, while creativity, we see, diminishes his ability to engage in a healthy love.

The psychologist Carl Rogers has declared that "the mainspring of creativity appears to be the same tendency which we discover so deeply as the curative force in psychotherapy—man's tendency to actualize himself, to become his potentialities."[4] Jeremy's art is indeed very much like psychotherapy, growing out of his attempt to create a psychological wholeness. But Jeremy has had no practice in integration outside of art, no practice in linking his art and his life, his conscious and his unconscious. His mother has given him only parts of a self that he has tried to put together.

We recall that his mother, who saved everything, had a habit of sending Jeremy's sisters Amanda and Laura news items stuffed in envelopes. Amanda always tried, in vain, to figure out the relevance of these clippings to her mother's letters and to her own life. In Mrs. Pauling and in Amanda we see the two parts of the process: saving fragments and putting them together. Jeremy brings the two processes together in his artwork, which he significantly calls "pieces." Amanda tells us: "He has had this drive to paste things together ever since he was old enough for scissors and a gluepot" (*CN* 23).

At the beginning of the novel, it is clear that Jeremy has managed this gluing process in his collages, but not in life. His inability to transfer what he knows from art to life recalls the "sharply split type" of the obsessive-compulsive personality that A. H. Maslow has described. According to Maslow, these obsessive-compulsives are, like Jeremy, split between "what they are conscious of, what they know about themselves, and what's concealed from themselves, what is unconscious or repressed." For this type, the way to safety is away from threat and anxiety.[5] Whatever is new is threatening; they are afraid of emotions. (Jeremy is especially afraid to face the realization that he actually hated his mother.) What Maslow says of this psychological type—"He's really fighting off dangers within himself"—we could say of Jeremy. If Jeremy breaks the line, bringing his conscious into contact with his unconscious, he may have to face his real feelings about his mother and his own unsatisfied needs. (And indeed, late in the novel, when Jeremy confronts his feelings about his mother and admits his own "errors of aimlessness, passivity, and echoing internal silence," he commits himself to an heroic plunge into the real, external world, acknowledging his need for Mary, putting on Abby's pink nylon backpack, and setting out to reconnect himself to his family [*CN* 252–53]. But it is a risk—both the contact with the world inside and outside—that he cannot sustain.)

Yet Jeremy is unlike the usual obsessive-compulsive in a significant way; it is a difference that makes him into an artist instead of a psychotic. Maslow's typical obsessive-compulsive "kills off and walls off everything unconscious in order to be sure that the dangerous portions of it don't get out." The portion of the unconscious typically denied is the part out of which, Maslow says, "comes the ability to play—to enjoy, to fantasy, to laugh, to loaf, to be spontaneous—and, what's most important for us here—creativity, which is a kind of intellectual play, which is a kind of permission to be ourselves, to fantasy, to let loose, and to be crazy, privately."[6] Jeremy has no playfulness, no spontaneity *in life* (we never hear him actually laugh), but this playful side of the self, lopped off from his lived reality, finds expression in his art.

But if Jeremy's art is a gesture toward achieving balance in his life, his way of dealing with psychological disequilibrium, it is an equilibrium gained at the price of great energy loss. His initial balance comes from his careful separation of the worlds of the conscious and the unconscious, with art as the only real point of contact between the two. The result in the beginning of the novel is expressed in the small frame of Jeremy's collages, in their one-dimensional glued-together bits and pieces. Reading about them, we scarcely need to be reminded of the premise of philosophers and theologians that the created resembles the Creator.[7] In fact, this art (only vaguely representational—"No definite outlines to them," Amanda sniffs [*CN* 24]) probably expresses in its lack of realistic content something like the true state of Jeremy's unconscious at the time: there is little in the way of a genuine encounter between his unconscious and the external world. Only in the physical artifacts of his creativity do the external and the internal meet for Jeremy.

Then, for a while, with Mary—his new, good mother (Mary, who moves into his mother's room; Mary, the mother of us all, whose color is blue; earth mother and cohort of the creator without benefit of marriage)— Jeremy manages another kind of balance between art and living. Because Mary and the children have touched his humanity so much more deeply and less threateningly than his mother did, they have blurred the barriers of his self-containment, leading Jeremy to a new artistic response, larger, literally, than his previous work. As he is brought into closer and closer contact with life, Jeremy's art moves into three-dimensions, taking on new texture and complexity, moving even to irony (although he seems not to be conscious of it) in the picture-perfect rose-covered cottage that makes Mary so uneasy. It is clear that the world has invaded his unconscious, and he projects that new union in his art.

Jeremy thinks of this expanded middle period of his life as like the wide part of an eye, a metaphor appropriate for his growing capacity to see the world outside his self and express his response to it. In this period, he comes closest to attaining a type of artistic balance involving some sort of communication between the conscious and the unconscious, between the relational and the artistic selves. He seems capable now both of integrating the details of his external life and his emotional response to that life and of alternating between the practical requirements of his life as a husband and father and his life as an artist. Indeed, his *modus vivendi* is like the one Tyler describes herself and her husband achieving, when they come out of a period of writing, her husband speaking in Persian, she acting "absent-minded and short-tempered," but coming out nevertheless, connecting nevertheless with their children and with life's ordinary demands.[8]

The new balance that Jeremy achieves is, however, a precarious one, easily thrown out of whack. Becoming overwhelmed by his domestic ties, Jeremy begins to dream of retreat. His new pain is different from his old; his new emptiness, larger, because it involves more complex repudiations. His art has more dimensions and greater texture now because his life has. The great irony is that what destroys Jeremy's venture into the world of the living are the demands inherent in the art that has grown and matured as a consequence of his venturing out of his psychological confinement.

Those artistic demands take a number of shapes. One cause of Jeremy's defeat as husband and father (as a full person living in the everyday world) is the concentration demanded by art. What Stephen Spender has said about writing poetry applies as well to other kinds of creation: "The problem of creative writing is essentially one of concentration, and the supposed eccentricities of poets are usually due to mechanical habits or rituals developed in order to concentrate."[9] Jeremy's concentration in his art is so total that it can be seen as a kind of psychological distillation. In the act of creating, he is reduced to one point of perception. (As Amanda says, "All his eye for detail goes into cutting and pasting. There is none left over for real life."[*CN* 24]) Spender describes creativity as a spiritual activity that results in the disturbance of the balance of the body and mind, causing the creator to forget that indeed he does have a body. As Jeremy becomes more and more concentrated in his art, there is less of a self to make available to his family.

It is as if Jeremy has but a finite amount of "self," a territory to be fought over and parceled out between the demands of life on the one hand and art on the other. An alternate model of creativity might suggest a relationship in which life and art mutually nourish each other, creating two wholenesses, accessible, at least in part, to each other—something like Jeremy at mid-novel. In the beginning of the novel and at the end, however, only a small part of Jeremy's self is engaged in life; the rest of Jeremy is totally concentrated on his art and is thus unavailable to living relationships. The sagging Jeremy on the stairs at the beginning and the whispering Jeremy at the end, "peaceful . . . distant, detached" (*CN* 276), bear witness to an artist whose works are literally his life. Olivia says that Jeremy "faded away as he worked, as if art erased him somehow. As if each piece were another layer scraped off him, when already he was down to the quick." (*CN* 232)

A second enemy of the relational self is also inherent in the model of the creator exemplified by Jeremy. Jeremy's very self-containment as an artist destines him to failure with Mary and the children. When the old boarder Mr. Somerset says, "He's not himself at all today," Jeremy's sister Amanda responds: "People say that about Jeremy quite often, but what they mean is that he is not like other people. He is *always* himself. That's what's wrong with him." (*CN* 13) And, humanly speaking, that *is* what's wrong with him.

In a further Tylerian irony, Jeremy thinks the same of Mary: that she is complete in herself. In fact, her maternal generativity parallels his artistic creativity. Each threatens the other with completeness; yet each needs the other as source of creation. In their own individual completeness, he and Mary defeat each other as a couple. Jeremy (compete in his art) and Mary (purposely self-sufficient in her childbearing and -rearing) form two perfect circles enclosing themselves and walling the other out. (Mary has been led to this psychological protection by her early failed marriage: "I learned my lesson the first time around. Women should never leave any vacant spots for the men to fill; they should form an unbroken circle on their own and enclose each child within it." [*CN* 197]) Jeremy knows intuitively the problem with the circle, at least as artistic form: in his collages, he finds that the blue circle is "difficult to work with. He [has] to cut it into angles" (*CN* 43), but he can't transfer this aesthetic insight into life.

Jeremy and Mary are both like gods (the creator god and the earth goddess), needing no other—or at least acting as if they need no other, resigned finally to their isolation. Jeremy mourns and then accepts the fact that "everybody *outside* me left" (*CN* 243). In the end, although we have only Miss Vinton's passing description of Jeremy's "great towering beautiful sculptures," we suspect that his art has returned to a non-representational expression of the unconscious self, enlarged now because of his growth through love and pain and loss, but no longer clearly connected with the world outside his own mind. Tyler suggests that Jeremy's and Mary's agony is that they have been fated by their own psychological compulsions to godlike self-sufficiency in spite of their human need to be less than complete, to break out of the circle of self, to be vulnerable to encounters with otherness. The human fall is once again triggered by a desire to be like the divine. But this time, for Jeremy, this is a fall *from* humanity—and it is a *felix culpa* only in terms of art. By the end of the novel Jeremy has become so godlike that he is the creator in retreat from the world, almost invisible except in his creations.

His art also gives Jeremy another godlike quality that diminishes his human connectedness: like the divine creator, Jeremy is outside of time. Mary thinks that he's "not really a product of his time. . . . Sometimes he seems younger than I am, as if events are what age people." (*CN* 215) In human terms, the timeless creator might as well be dead—as Jeremy very nearly is dead to real life in the end. Macon Leary arrives at this insight in *The Accidental Tourist* when he learns that what makes the dead "so heart-breaking" is their immunity to time: "The real adventure, he thought, is the flow of time; it's as much adventure as anyone could wish" (*AT* 354).

And that is the adventure that Jeremy misses. Perhaps, however, his timelessness is the price he pays for his art. Or perhaps it is one of the sources of his creativity. Not tied to his time, he can, in effect, see all time; freed from detail, he can perceive the larger, abstract reality. Miss Vinton comes close to understanding this when she says of one of Jeremy's sculptures:

> "This man with the rake, slightly stooped and motionless, reminded me that life is nothing *but* motion and passes too swiftly for us to observe with the naked eye. At least, for me to observe. Jeremy has no trouble whatsoever. He sees from a distance at all times, without trying, even trying not to. It is his condition. He *lives* at a distance. He makes pictures the way other men make maps—setting down the new fixed points that he knows, hoping they will guide him as he goes floating through this unfamiliar planet. He keeps his eyes on the horizon while his hands work blind." (*CN* 145)

The celestial navigation that makes for his strength in art, makes for his weakness in living.

And yet a final characteristic inherent in Jeremy's art is inimicable to life. Like his mother, Jeremy is almost totally a receiver. Mrs. Pauling, when pregnant, "had room for only one person at a time": ". . . while she was expecting Jeremy, she curled more and more inside herself until she was only a kind of circular hollow taking in nourishment and asking for afghans . . . a receiver" (*CN* 17). Jeremy takes the children's mittens and caps; he takes Brian's running from the house; and finally, in what Olivia calls his "time machine," he takes all the bits and pieces of the family life together—from Rachel's baby spoon to Pippi's plastic banana. But Jeremy does not become exactly like his mother; he makes a return. What he gives back, of course, is the art itself. This, however, is a return to capital-letter *Life* and not to the child whose mitten was scavenged or the wife whose dress and heart were used up in the making of the work of art.

If these are the demands of art—total concentration, self-sufficiency, imperviousness to time, and complete receptivity to what life offers one's art (without any sense of a reciprocal obligation)—perhaps it is understandable why characters in other of Tyler's novels have turned to art's less demanding offspring: craft. So Elizabeth carves her wooden figures in *The Clock Winder;* Ezra leaves his flute for cooking in *Dinner at the Homesick Restaurant;* Charlotte takes up photography in *Earthly Possessions;* and Macon Leary drops his collegiate attempts at poetry to write those travel guides in *The Accidental Tourist.* Perhaps there is a reminder here that often human connectedness (even the tenuous connections made by these characters) is achieved at the sacrifice of the possibility of high levels of creativity.

Celestial Navigation may be, as much as anything, a tribute to the person whose fate is the opposite, who sacrifices life for art. Jeremy's triumph is that he does manage to turn the pieces of his existence into art. That he never manages to reverse the process and make his life into a whole as well may offer yet another reminder that people who sail with the gods can seldom determine their own destinations or feel at home again in human ports.

NOTES

1. In *The Writer on Her Work,* ed. Janet Sternburg (New York: Norton, 1980), p. 9.
2. Wassily Kandinsky, "The Doctrine of Internal Necessity," in *Creativity in the Arts,* ed. Vincent Tomas (Englewood Cliffs, N.J.: Prentice-Hall, 1964), p. 50.
3. "The Psychology of Imagination," in *A Source Book for Creative Thinking,* ed. Sidney J. Parnes and Harold F. Harding (New York: Charles Scribner's Sons, 1962), p. 237.
4. "Toward a Theory of Creativity," in *A Source Book,* pp. 65–66.
5. "Emotional Blocks to Creativity," in *A Source Book,* p. 96.
6. Ibid.
7. Etienne Gilson, "Creation—Artistic, Natural, and Divine," in *Creativity in the Arts,* p. 61.
8. "Still Just Writing," in *The Writer on Her Work,* p. 9.
9. "The Making of a Poem," in *Creativity in the Arts,* p. 35.

The Effects of the
Artistic Process:
A Study of Three Artist Figures
in Anne Tyler's Fiction

SUE LILE INMAN

F or me, writing something down was the only road out," Anne Tyler
declares in her essay, "Still Just Writing."[1] What she writes down,
however, is not confessional autobiography. Her private life and her
life as an artist Tyler protects, refusing the lecture circuit, the *Today Show,*
and most interviews. She claims that a principal reason for writing is to lead
more lives than one. And so, in her eleven novels, she filters the observed
world through her comic sensibility, what she has called a "mist of irony,"[2]
and directs our focus to particular people, ordinary people who are afraid to
leave home, who sell hardware, who run restaurants; and we come to
recognize, in her idiosyncratic characters, life as it is actually lived in the
last part of the twentieth century. As her characters dramatize their lives,
reveal their own thoughts, show how they see one another, Tyler remains
the self-effacing artist hidden behind them.

Careful scrutiny of her artist figures, however, makes it possible to
glimpse Tyler's view of what happens to the artist swept up in the artistic
process, and to those close to the artist. Three such artist characters are
Jeremy Pauling, the agoraphobic visual artist of *Celestial Navigation;*
Morgan Gower, the eccentric impostor who cannot resist "stepping into
other people's worlds," passing for a physician, a street priest, and other

roles for which he costumes himself in *Morgan's Passing;* and from *Dinner at the Homesick Restaurant,* Ezra Tull, hardly a conventional artist, who loves to feed people what they need to eat according to his sense of how they feel. Tyler's narrative techniques—the choice of viewpoint and what she chooses to dramatize in the lives of these artists—reveal the costly effects of being possessed by the creative process.

In Jeremy Pauling we see, as Tyler says, the artist's "tendency to turn more and more inward."[3] The story develops over a long period of time, from 1960 to 1973, a span of time, characteristic of Tyler's mature fiction, that fits precisely the slow response time of this protagonist. She alternates viewpoint: the women around Jeremy narrate their sections in first person, but the Jeremy sections are told in third person limited, a narrative technique that respects Jeremy's distant, reclusive nature and his huge interior silent center.

The novel is carefully constructed within a frame with Jeremy's persnickety sister Amanda introducing us to Jeremy through her scornful viewpoint at the time of their mother's funeral (the prologue) and the closing very brief epilogue told from Miss Vinton's viewpoint in 1973. From the moment Jeremy meets Mary Tell, the runaway wife who moves into the Pauling boardinghouse with her daughter, Tyler dramatizes the interplay between art and life—the effects of one on the other. Jeremy has been constructing two-dimensional collages from the bits and pieces of life around him; after he meets Mary, he grows restless with his work's flatness, and begins gradually to add depth and texture. As Doris Betts has pointed out, this added depth and texture parallel Tyler's statement that being a wife and mother has given her own creative work more dimension.[4] In the course of the novel, we see also the effects of the artistic process on Jeremy Pauling's life. He lives life at a distance; he admits the twentieth century has been lost on him, as he works in his third story studio above and removed from the noisy household of six children (he and Mary have five together).

Mary is the kind of woman found frequently in Tyler's novels—nurturing, practical, adapting easily to the clutter and fretfulness of a growing family. She is "earthbound" and therefore the consummate Other for Jeremy; as long as he and she remain engaged, intimately connected, he is able to resist turning totally inward, being absolutely possessed by the creative process. Miss Vinton, the spinster boarder who has real affection for them both yet always maintains a discreet respectful distance, sees that he travels by "celestial navigation." As a creature of the air, Jeremy needs the earthbound Mary, but once Mary focuses too much on his weakness, his vulnerability, and ceases to ask for his help in going to the hospital when she is about to give birth, then their balanced connection is broken and is never set right again. She removes her need for him in her obsessive desire to be self-sufficient and in her sympathy for his fear of leaving home, but in so doing, he is abandoned to his fear and weakness and to the all-consuming effects of creating art. He turns more inward, more forgetful of time, more neglectful of his own basic needs for food and rest.

When Mary's divorce becomes final and she and Jeremy are free to marry (after having lived together as married for ten years), she tells him they can get married on Thursday. The reader knows Jeremy is too much occupied by his art to take in the news. All sense of time is lost in his obsession with his new work. Ironically, he is building a sculpture of a man running from his responsibilities, inspired by the sight from his third floor window of Brian, his gallery dealer, leaving Jeremy's house after a vain attempt to talk to him. Jeremy sees him happy to be fleeing and must capture that moment. He works in a steady trance, with growing elation. All the time he is cutting and curling tin strips for the statue's hair, the reader can never quite forget what day it is, what Mary must be feeling, though Tyler keeps the narrative focus on Jeremy in the studio. His total absorption in whatever appears luminous in his peculiar field of vision takes precedence over any other consideration, his art work expressing what he cannot—his soul's resistance to intimacy. He forgets to meet the mother of his children on their wedding day. (And the irony doubles because Jeremy, on studying his sculpture later, is dissatisfied with the creation, sees that it does not match his interior vision, and takes apart what he has made.)

When Jeremy discovers that no lunch has been obligingly placed outside his studio, he wakes up to everyday consciousness and goes downstairs. The sight of the shiny clean kitchen, the smooth unslept-in beds, the stillness with only a clock ticking bring the sure sense that his entire family could have been gone for thirty years. This scene creates vividly the effect of timelessness upon the artist and the fear that every artist must feel, the dread that while he is immersed in creative work, he will be abandoned by those he loves. Jeremy returns to his studio and his work like a forlorn old man, but he also feels relieved to be alone, no longer subject to interruptions. He stands, perplexed, wondering, "What is it I have been waiting to do?" (*CN* 189) Thus, Anne Tyler dramatizes the ambivalence within the artist toward his family. The artistic process exacts a dear price from the artist and from those who live with the artist.

The effects on Mary and the six children are emblemized by the dilapidated shack in which they take up residence, in the spring of 1971. Expecting Jeremy to read her note on the refrigerator and come for them immediately, she at first assumes they will not be there long. In her retaliation for his ignoring their marriage ceremony and in her determination to become self-sufficient, she has disregarded Jeremy's very nature: how slowly he takes in everyday reality, how painful such a trip would be for him, how rejected he would feel and yet relieved at no longer being interrupted constantly.

Without the ballast that Mary provided, Jeremy has no one holding him to everyday reality. Tyler uses another woman character to dramatize Jeremy's extreme state of mind. Olivia, the anorexic runaway Mary has befriended, takes it upon herself to show the world that she understands Jeremy in a way that Mary never could, that she can be *inside* his mind with him. In her fantasy she becomes convinced that she will inspire the great artist to create masterpieces. For a while she watches him in his studio, but before long they sit for hours immobile in front of TV game shows and finally lie like corpses in a catatonic state on the bed, completely out of touch, until Miss Vinton demands that Olivia take note of what is happening, that she has allowed Jeremy to become too removed.

It is not until Olivia has gone away, that Jeremy rises out of the abyss. In despair he wonders, "Wasn't there anything to lift him out of this stillness inside?" (*CN* 252) He finds instruction for what to do next only through art. As he had ten years earlier when he wanted to court Mary and recalled the way romantic novels treated courtship, so now he remembers that in literature there is a necessary journey: "He had a vague longing to undertake some metaphysical task, to make some pilgrimage" (*CN* 252). By this time, it is November 1971, and Mary Tell and the children are preparing Brian's shack by the river for winter. When Jeremy Pauling makes the trip by bus, his child's pink nylon backpack loaded with a sandwich and the ludicrous surprise toys he has purchased at Woolworth's, we cheer him for this act of courage; the trip is a heroic undertaking for Jeremy. The scene of Jeremy's caulking the windows with newspaper and tape for Mary becomes a poignant scene of two people at cross purposes, seen from the respectful but compassionate distance Anne Tyler provides for us. As Jeremy makes the dangerous journey in the dinghy to air the sails on Brian's boat, we are left there with him, sick with the knowledge that his courageous pilgrimage has failed to bring him the fulfillment of love met and re-won.

In the epilogue, he is back in the boardinghouse, looked after by Miss Vinton, who knows that he must leave his studio from time to time and walk with her to the grocery store, in order to stay in touch with everyday life. His female counterpart now is a separate and distinct Other, but without the emotional connection Mary gave him. Being engulfed by the artistic process has cost him intimacy, and protected him from intimacy, as his art literally and metaphorically has taken on more and more size and dimension until his towering sculptures dwarf ordinary life.

Morgan Gower, an apparent opposite to Jeremy, loves nothing better than to escape his home—a houseful of women (seven daughters, his wife Bonny, his senile mother, and his neurotic sister), and to escape his humdrum job in a rundown hardware store. In *Morgan's Passing,* the artist protagonist turns outward. He walks around Baltimore, assuming different identities. Anne Tyler plays out in Morgan Gower the motivation she has expressed as her own: to lead more lives than one. Tyler has said, *"Morgan's Passing* deals with a situation I've been fascinated by for most of my life, and one which probably is not unrelated to being a writer: the inveterate impostor, who is unable to stop himself from stepping into other people's worlds."[5] In him, Tyler explores the artist's imaginative entry into other people's lives and the effect of such obsession on the artist's own identity.

Reviewers have criticized *Morgan's Passing* for being less carefully structured than her other novels; they have seen it as fragmentary. Frank Shelton has called it "unruly and untidy."[6] More to the point, however, Tyler has again suited the form to the character she is exploring. Morgan takes up projects (writing a science fiction novel, restringing a banjo) and drops them; he moves from posing as an endearing Polish immigrant to a street priest blessing store owners. He may be a convincing artist at improvisation, but he is also an undisciplined, easily distracted artist, who for years has kept all his different worlds separate from his "real" one. So the narrative fragments that trace Morgan's passage through a dozen years, from 1967 to 1979, suit her subject exactly. As does her choice of viewpoint.

In the beginning, Tyler uses a narrator's matter-of-fact, reporting voice to describe a puppet show of Cinderella that ends abruptly with Cinderella slumping over, a young man calling for a doctor, children asking, "Is it over?" (*MP* 5) A bearded man in a pointy ski cap appears, delivers Emily and Leon Meredith's baby in the backseat of his car, and, when the ambulance reaches the hospital, he disappears. The viewpoint is objective reporting, whereby the reader learns only what an outside observer would see of Morgan and is taken in by his artistry, as the Merediths are. But in the second section, labeled the next year, 1968, the narrator addresses the reader directly: "You could say he was a man who had gone to pieces, or maybe he'd always been in pieces; maybe he'd arrived unassembled" (*MP* 23). The point of view accomplishes several artistic goals at once. While depicting segments of Morgan's life that never touch one another, Tyler assures the reader that there is a narrator in charge, that the story itself is under control. And letting the strings show as artist-manipulator, an unusual act for Tyler, matches her focus on the imaginative artist as creator and manipulator of other lives.

But not far into the 1968 section, Tyler closes the distance and moves into the characters' limited vision, thoughts, and feelings. The rare glimpse of Tyler's puppetry has served its purpose; now the characters take over to reveal themselves and their lives. For the rest of the story, Tyler alternates the third-person viewpoint between Morgan and Emily. At one point, late in the story, after Emily and Morgan have married, Emily lies in bed, reflecting on her new life with "this bearded man, this completely other person. She felt drawn to him by something far outside herself—by strings that pulled her, by ropes." (*MP* 270) The statement expresses Emily's consciousness of their opposite natures being inexorably drawn together as if by fate while it subtly reminds the reader of the novelist's control.

Morgan watches and follows and imagines what it must be like to be Emily and Leon Meredith. He creates his idea of the Merediths and is utterly convinced that the way he envisions their life is the way it is and has to be. He sees the constancy and simplicity in Emily's choice of clothing—her black leotard and skirt—and deduces that their life is as uncluttered and spare. He loves to say they are itinerate puppeteers. Emily says to him any number of times, "We're not who you believe we are" (*MP* 116). Emily and Leon resist Morgan's creation of them. In her essay, "Because I Want More Than One Life," Tyler describes the resistance of characters who refuse to do what their creator invents for them. "Every new attempt ends up in the wastebasket, until I'm forced to admit it: The characters just won't allow this. I'll have to let the plot go their way. And when I do, everything falls into place."[7] An essential part of the creative process is recognizing the stubborn integrity of what is being created; the effect on the artist is frustration until he yields. Tyler asks, "Where did those little paper people get so much power?"[8] When Morgan enters fully into the Merediths' life, supplanting Leon, and brings his worlds together in his life with Emily, new life is created, literally, in Joshua their baby, and in his role with Emily as itinerate puppeteer for the Holy Word Entertainment Troupe.

But the cost to Emily is dear. Just as those associated with Jeremy and his art pay dearly, so Emily experiences deep loss. She loses her daughter, Gina, to Leon. He claims that Emily's life with Morgan (and his senile mother and crazy sister) is unstable. (Morgan asks her, "How can you have a more stable life than ours?" [*MP* 277])

Beneath the surface of *Morgan's Passing* is the mystery of identity. Morgan Gower, in his outrageous costumes and hats, moves in and out of roles, settling finally as himself with Emily but known to his employer as Leon Meredith, and then his ex-wife Bonny publishes his obituary as a joke that actually works to free her to remarry and retain her dignity, without the stigma of desertion and divorce. Bonny's action upsets Morgan enough to break his compulsion (at least for a moment) to assume whatever identity people suppose him to have. In an almost throwaway scene, he answers the phone and automatically tells the wrong number that yes, he is "Sam" but stops himself, in a dizzying moment of rebalancing: "I'm not Sam. Please. You have the wrong number." (*MP* 300) For the first time, Morgan refuses a false identity.

The art of role-playing, of living more than one life, requires that the artist cross boundaries separating himself from others. But psychologists tell us that a strong sense of identity depends upon a respect for boundaries, the most primitive boundary being between self and other. Morgan has never regarded boundaries seriously—he's actually a bigamist, having married when he was quite young and never having bothered to obtain a divorce before he posed as a suitor-with-promise and asked Bonny's wealthy father for her hand. The effect of his unbounded imagination and exuberant artistry shows up in his sorrowful admission to Emily and Leon: "I tend to think . . . that nothing real has ever happened to me, but when I look back I see that I'm wrong . . . . but somehow it's as if this were all a story, just something that happened to somebody else." (*MP* 210–211)

Morgan may question his own reality, but Emily knows him and so does the reader. His identity remains true and constant, as constant really as Emily's and her black leotard and wrap skirt. Emily reflects on how seeing a blown up photograph of "Wilbur Wright poised on the sand at Kitty Hawk—capped and suited, strangely stylish, suspended forever in that tense, elated, ready position—reminded her for some reason of Morgan" (*MP* 213). Anne Tyler has said that she doubts people actually change very much.[9] Such a belief in the constancy of a person's essence gives the theme of identity that undergirds this novel about a man who takes up identities and drops them a decided ironic resonance. Morgan's artistry affects his perception of himself, but the reader is left with the sure conviction of who Morgan is. For all his outward role-playing, he remains the exuberant man of boundless imagination and curiosity, with an eye for the believable detail, one who always sees possibilities ahead.

The question of identity plays itself out quite differently in *Dinner at the Homesick Restaurant*. Unlike Morgan, the artist figure here, Ezra Tull, practices his art in a manner so self-effacing and natural, he does not draw attention to himself. Tyler's narrative technique in this her ninth novel shows mastery of both the novel and the short story forms. The ten chapters, each titled and each with a particular member of the Tull family as the focal character, could have been discrete short stories with their own rising action and pivotal moments, yet they are arranged to build in suspense as Tyler plumbs deeper and deeper into the shaft of memory from Pearl Tull's deathbed at age 85 to mine the vein of Beck Tull's desertion of his family, Pearl's abusive temper, the compulsive competitiveness and jealousy of the oldest child, Cody, the steady endurance of the stay-at-home son Ezra, and the cheerful management of family and pediatric practice of Pearl's daughter, Jenny. As Benjamin DeMott says of *Dinner at the Homesick Restaurant,* "It is a border crossing"[10] because of its wisdom. Tyler, the self-effacing artist herself, presents each person's story without intrusion and with such compassion, it is impossible to despise any of them despite Pearl's cruelty, Cody's betrayal, Ezra's passivity, or Jenny's protective distance.

Tyler's deftness and mastery show up in her portrayal of Ezra. Most of what we learn about him comes through the words and actions of the other characters. Pearl thinks of him: "so sweet and clumsy it could break your heart . . . his calm face that she loved to linger on" (*DHR* 4,5). Tyler solves the problem of how to present Ezra, a good-natured, unself-conscious person, and make him believable by focusing on him through Cody's negative viewpoint. The more winsome Ezra becomes, happily playing "The Ash Grove" on his reed whistle, the more furious Cody grows in his resentment, convinced as he is that Ezra is his mother's favorite. As a child, Cody plays dirty tricks on his younger brother; as an adult, he schemes and marries Ruth, the scrawny red-haired cook Ezra intended to marry, as Pearl says, the only thing he has ever wanted. Through Cody's observation, we learn the way Ezra works in his art form, feeding people in his restaurant: "Ezra was so impervious—so thickheaded, really; nothing ever touched him . . . . He liked anything that was offered him, especially bread . . . . But above all else, he was a feeder. He would set a dish before you and then stand there with his face expectant . . . . There was something tender, almost loving, about his attitude toward people who were eating what he'd cooked them." (*DHR* 161) Cody remembers when Pearl had asked Ezra why he wouldn't stand up to the neighborhood bully, and Ezra had said, "I'm trying to get through life as a liquid" (*DHR* 166). Cody, who was trying to get through life as a rock, had laughed. Tyler's use of strong contrast between Cody and Ezra imprints Ezra's unassuming nature upon our minds.

Ezra's art is an integral part of his nature, an outgrowth of it. He is a nurturer, who moves from his instinctive sense of others' needs to his creative work, cooking just the food he believes they should have to satisfy them. He responds to the deprivation of nurture he experienced as a child in Pearl's household by creating a homey place to eat, transforming Mrs. Scarlatti's elegant place for formal dining into the Homesick Restaurant.

With no authorial intrusion, Tyler dramatizes the effect a protege may have upon his artist mentor and sponsor through Ezra's aggressive destruction of Mrs. Scarlatti's fine restaurant. As an artist, his vision of what he wants is sure. Showing none of the passivity he exhibits in his relationships, Ezra rips out the walls, destroying all barriers that would separate the kitchen from the dinner guests. He does not hesitate out of any consideration for his mentor's feelings. He knows she expects him to take over the restaurant after she dies, yet he cannot wait until her death but acts while she is in the hospital, expected to die. When she recovers and sees what he has done, she is shocked and dismayed, demanding that her name be removed from the restaurant. Her response dramatizes the sense of betrayal the mentor often experiences when the artist he has trained and nurtured expresses his own individual vision.

In contrast to Jeremy, whose art protects him from intimacy, Ezra tries relentlessly through the artistic process to bring his family together at splendid dinners he creates in the hope that they will be close and loving as he supposes normal families are. Instead, the Tulls never complete one of the dinners at the Homesick Restaurant; one or another will throw down his napkin and storm out in a huff. The final person to break up a dinner is Beck Tull, who has returned after thirty-five years to attend Pearl's funeral. There is the hope held out at the end that perhaps the Tulls will at last finish a meal together. When Cody finds his father and they make an uneasy peace, it is Cody who suggests, "Let's go finish our dinner" (*DHR* 302).

Ezra Tull illustrates the unself-conscious artist, who as a child plays his whistle and as an adult runs the restaurant, riding out the irrational rages of his mother, the disappointment of losing his fiancee to his domineering brother, the griefs and despair of middle age. While Tyler shows that the artistic process may exact a dear price from the artist and those surrounding the artist and that art is limited in its power to change people's lives, or their ability to love, she also allows us to see that art done with love can be a way to survive, to endure.

NOTES

1. In *The Writer on Her Work,* ed. Janet Sternburg (New York: Norton, 1980), p. 15.

2. Ibid., p. 12.

3. Mary Ellen Brooks, "Anne Tyler," *Dictionary of Literary Biography,* vol. 6: *American Novelists since World War II, Second Series,* ed. James E. Kibler, Jr. (Detroit: Gale Research, 1980), 341.

4. "The Fiction of Anne Tyler," *The Southern Quarterly,* 21 (4) (Summer 1983), 30–31.

5. Brooks, p. 344.

6. "The Necessary Balance: Distance and Sympathy in the Novels of Anne Tyler," *Southern Review,* 20 (4) (Autumn 1984), 855.

7. *Washington Post,* 15 August 1976, sec. G, p. 7.

8. Ibid.

9. Cited in "The Fiction of Anne Tyler," p. 26.

10. "Funny, Wise and True" [rev. of *Dinner at the Homesick Restaurant*], *The New York Times Book Review,* 14 March 1982, p. 1.

Morgan's Passion

GORDON O. TAYLOR

*It was only acting, but who knows: sometimes you act like a certain
person long enough, you become that person. Wasn't it possible?*
                                                    —*Morgan's Passing*

Early in Anne Tyler's *Morgan's Passing*—published in 1980, the
eighth of her eleven novels to date—Morgan Gower sits in the kitch-
en of his cluttered Baltimore house, perusing the personals in the
classified ads. "LOST. *White wedding dress, size 10. No questions asked,*" he
reads to himself, a smile slowly forming around his cigarette, as questions
begin to take shape in his mind. "LOST. *Upper denture. Great sentimental
value,*" he states aloud to his wife Bonny as she enters the room, adding "I
made it up about the sentimental value," to which she replies with soft
derision that she never would have guessed, having heard him spin elaborate fictions out of such bits and pieces of fact before. "Hmm? Listen to
this," Morgan murmurs to the world at large, "hitting his stride" (in Tyler's
phrase):

> M.G. *All is not forgiven and never will be.*
>   Bonny set a cup of coffee in front of him.
>   "What if that's me?" Morgan asked.
>   "What if that's you?"
>   "M.G. Morgan Gower."
>   "Did you do something unforgivable?"
>   "You can't help wondering," Morgan said, "seeing a thing like that. You
> can't help stopping to think." (*MP* 31–32)

Morgan reads the personals—and the help wanteds, and the obituaries and the rest—because he can't help wondering at the glimpses they afford into the private lives of others, mysterious realms the "reality" of which consists in their resistance, as well as their availability, to his own narrative recastings of them, rather than merely in their exposure to the voracity of his voyeuristic eye.

Like the housefronts and storefronts Morgan watches from the windows of the buses he rides through Baltimore neighborhoods—giving the illusion of a turning world to the still point of his restless imagination—these lives into which he peers, into which he often *dis*appears, are at once his confident creations and the agencies of his own precarious existence. As such they can threaten, even as they promise to disguise or transform, his personal being. Indeed, toward the end of the novel Morgan comes across his own obituary, placed by his wife for reasons both obvious and obscure, a report of his passing greatly exaggerated (as Mark Twain would have it), but not in all respects untrue.

Morgan's response to the personal notice seemingly addressed to him— "M.G. *All is not forgiven and never will be*"—however playful, is not without its note of anxiety, as much in his question ("What if that's me?") as in his quizzical answer to Bonny's question of him ("Did you do something unforgivable?"). Conversely, his reaction to reading his obituary, however distressed, is not without its note of readiness to begin what by this time he regards as his new life, with a new family and perhaps a new name, each to his mind more an extension than a rejection of the old. In more ways than one, then—including if not limited to that of the artist's appropriation of experience, the experience thus refashioned becoming in turn a new part of an old, unalterable reality—Morgan Gower takes things personally. For Tyler the risk in this of his doing "something unforgivable" lies close to something else, something deeply and desirably human as well as outrageous in its presumption, capable of cruelty as certainly as it is informed by love; something similar to the power of art, suggestive as well of the power of *her* art.

The plot of *Morgan's Passing,* in its most conventional and least interesting sense, was summarized as follows in a review much less unsympathetic to the novel than such a précis, in its elision, might suggest:

> A young girl-wife [Emily] goes into labor while she and her boy-husband [Leon] are putting on a puppet-show of Cinderella at a church fair in Baltimore in 1967. Her baby is delivered en route to the hospital by a member of the audience [Morgan] who claims to be a doctor . . . . The fake doctor—who lives in a tumultuous, hopelessly cluttered house with an imperturbable wife [Bonny], seven daughters, his half-senile mother, and crackpot sister—attaches himself to the young couple and their child, following them, popping up at odd moments. Later [the bulk of the novel is here subsumed], after they

have all become friends [the heart of the novel lies in the gradually rendered plausibility of the seeming absurdity], this attachment narrows, focusing upon the young wife, with unsettling consequences for everyone.[1]

Inauspicious, to be sure. But even in this there are hints as to where the "story" more importantly resides, not so much "later" as in the different directions of "unsettling consequence" to Morgan's metamorphic "passing" into and through these other lives, veering in and out of his own. The review as a whole, along with others more often mixed in response to the book's strangeness than overridingly favorable or unfavorable, is not without a sense of the interplay of puppetry—the art and the science of the puppets themselves, in addition to their use in dramatic portrayals—with the characters' experience, and with the ambiguities of manipulation and control. The reviewer at least intimates the aesthetic delicacies and psychological intensities of resonance between the fairy tales thus dramatized and Tyler's representations of her characters' emotional being, the psychic stuff, after all, from which fairy tales spring, in their adult as well as their juvenile aspect. There is a sense of the subtlety with which major and minor figures alike are shown on the one hand as inescapably caught in the webs, immersed in the generational flow, of family, and on the other as able—especially in the cases of Morgan and Emily—not so much to break free as to extend the range of their imprisoning humanity in new and surprising directions. There is also a sensitivity to the oddly moving alchemies of feeling through which Morgan and Emily are drawn together, for good and ill to themselves and others, shifting the relational orbits of all concerned. Unlike some, this review acknowledges the novel's comic energy, peculiarly hospitable to a brooding pessimism with which, like the shade of trees in the wind, the book's concluding sense of life's "luminous possibilities" is dappled. Most of all, an attempt to encompass *Morgan's Passing* should begin and end—as some of the initial commentaries did—with a sense of the narrative as surging out from, and subsiding back into, Morgan's relentless reactivity to the world, as it is and as it might be, these shown as confused more often than clarified in relation to one another.

In this *Morgan's Passing* resembles Tyler's other novels, in which "plot" is the merest pretext or catalyst for the vastly more powerful determinations—and liberations—of "character." As Henry James put it, "What is character but the determination of incident? What is incident but the illustration of character?"[2] Personality is for Tyler at once closely bound by social circumstance and family history (most of all by family, what Joyce Carol Oates calls the "chains of blood and love"[3]), and utterly free. It is astonishing in its resilience, as well as in its capacity for unpredictable self-revision, which then falls back under the sway of the resilient world, renewing the cycle. In effect, Tyler says in all her work what Grace Paley's narrator says in "A Conversation with My Father": "Everyone, real or invented, deserves the open destiny of life."[4] This is not to say that in the work of either writer the destiny of life is necessarily open, or that people always get what they deserve. It *is*, however, to suggest that in Tyler's fiction, as in Paley's, the phrase "real or invented" should be understood as a single adjective—"real-or-invented," perhaps "real-*and*-invented"—applicable to "everyone," rather than as referring to alternative categories into which people or possibilities can be sorted, in Baltimore or in a book.

Certainly a sense of the world as subject to reinvention—randomly, from its own flux, as much as by anyone's deliberate plan—both forms and *in*-forms Morgan's attitudes and behavior, even as such revisions of reality turn out (like gears only momentarily slipped) to engage anew and be driven by the "actual" world's ongoing pressures. In this he resembles numerous other characters in Tyler's fictions, figures whose improvisations of self—active or *reactive*, purposeful or passive—negotiate the space between "real or invented," breaking and reforging this distinction in the process, slipping over from *or* into *and,* only there to discover a new set of limiting (as well as "luminously" enabling) possibilities: Jeremy Pauling in *Celestial Navigation,* or Mary Tell in the same book, making (or "telling," self-narrating) her way in a world from which Jeremy, himself an artist, retreats; Jenny or Cody Tull in *Dinner at the Homesick Restaurant,* or indeed their brother Ezra, dreaming a family history as distant from their own, yet also as proximate, as a parallel universe; Muriel Pritchett in *The Accidental Tourist,* adaptably at ease with the strangeness of a world she has never seen, or Macon Leary in the same work, strangely determined never to see the world he travels and of which he writes; Elizabeth Abbott in *The Clock Winder,* or Maggie Moran in *Breathing Lessons,* meddlers in the lives of others (Morgan Gower is nothing if not a meddler), but still more strikingly meddlers in their own.

Morgan, like most of Tyler's protagonists, refuses confinement to a single identity or role, the world a huge "help wanted" sign to which he responds as his many hats and costumes aid and abet him, and as the shifting situation requires, a figment of his own imagination, a puppet to his own puppeteer. So too *Morgan's Passing,* like most of Tyler's novels, refuses consignment to the critical categories thus far usually proposed in consideration of her work. It may also be that in her work in general she does not fully "translate" into established terms of academic discussion, although a certain amount of formal scholarship is accumulating, along with accumulations of broader critical and popular response, in print or on conference panels. Whether or not she should be expected so to "translate," eventually or ever, is another matter, itself by now part of the critical issue.

She is, and is not, the writer John Updike saw, in his review of *Morgan's Passing,* as seeking "the Southern ambience,"[5] or the writer whom Reynolds Price, who taught her while she was an undergraduate at Duke, has since called "the nearest thing we have to an urban Southern novelist."[6] She is, and is not, the "domestic novelist, one of that great line descending from Jane Austen," described by Edward Hoagland in his notice of *Breathing Lessons*.[7] Surely she is a gifted comic novelist, yet comparisons with, say, Alison Lurie—whose work has also been likened to that of Jane Austen—seem irrelevant and unilluminating of the novels of either. Gail Godwin's praise for *Celestial Navigation*,[8] while richly deserved, perhaps as usefully expressed the reviewing author's concerns as it defined those of the writer under review.

Tyler's fiction is "contemporary" in literary-technical performance, but in ways deflecting rather than inviting distinctions between the "modern" and various species of the "postmodern." In the case of *Morgan's Passing,* it would take a series of subtle, rather than drastic, adjustments of internal reference and narrative procedure to persuade us that the story takes place in, say, the 1940s or 1950s, rather than in the late 1960s and during the 1970s, or indeed that the book itself was written in another time.[9] Tyler speaks freely of the writers who have influenced her—Eudora Welty, for example—yet such acknowledgments tend to speak to general attitudes or dispositions, rather than to particular representational qualities. Of Welty she has said that "Reading her taught me there were stories to be written about the mundane life around me,"[10] and that "Reading [her] when I was growing up showed me that very small things are often really larger than the large things."[11] One thinks again of Paley, in *Enormous Changes at the Last Minute,* but also of Emily Dickinson's lines, "The Missing All—prevented Me/From missing minor Things,"[12] the question of Tyler's temporal, or temperamental, "location" in a constellation of writers contemporary or classical at once compelling and, perhaps by design, unclear.

She is of course a "Baltimore" novelist, but that too is an insufficient designation, however crucial Baltimore may be as the setting of most of her books. Her treatment of the city is grittily realistic, filled with past and present detail, Tyler no less than Morgan a relentless wanderer of neighborhoods, a devourer of scenes and semioticist of signs (commercial as well as more abstractly "textual"), melting into the immediacy of the city's ebb and flow, a stranger in a strange land. Yet this intransigent place, like the persons in it in the case of *Morgan's Passing,* slips easily and often, of its own accord, into the palpably insubstantial contours of a mysterious reality always just below the surface. If Los Angeles is for Alison Lurie "The Nowhere City" (the title of an early Lurie novel), Baltimore is for Tyler a "somewhere" town, in the sense of the thickening concretions of its specificities, but also in the sense of its masking, as well as intimating through the mask, a world elsewhere; the skull beneath the skin, but also the Beauty within the Beast. Tyler's Baltimore is a city "real or invented," allowing no choice between the two, insisting that the phrase contains a spectrum of possibilities within which one might, at any moment, become lost.

Consider an early passage in which Morgan, during one of his bus rides, absorbs and is absorbed by the urban environment (for Morgan a bus is the inverse equivalent of Clark Kent's phone booth, the transformational space within which he gives up his "real" identity in order to salvage, more than to save, the world):

> They passed more stores and office buildings. They whizzed through a corner of Morgan's old neighborhood, with most of the windows boarded up and trees growing out of caved-in roofs. (It had not done well without him.) Here were the Arbeiter Mattress Factory and Madam Sheba, All Questions Answered and Love Problems Cheerfully Solved. Rowhouses slid by, each more decayed than the one before. Morgan hunkered in his seat, clutching the metal bar in front of him, gazing at the Ace of Spades Sandwich Shop and Fat Boy's Shoeshine. Now he was farther downtown than he had ever lived. He relaxed his grip on the metal bar. He sank into the lives of the scattered people sitting on their stoops: the woman in her nightgown and vinyl jacket nursing a Rolling Rock beer and breathing frost; the two men nudging each other and laughing; the small boy in a grownup's sneakers hugging a soiled white cat. A soothing kind of emptiness began to spread through him. He felt stripped and free, like the vacant windows, frameless, glassless, on the upper floors of Syrenia's Hot Pig Bar-B-Q. (*MP* 38–39)

Maybe this is just another mid-life crisis—Morgan is passing into his fifties. Perhaps, more hauntingly, this "emptiness" is related to the fact of his father's suicide, toward which Morgan turns in memory, diving into the wreck of the past in hope of resurfacing in the present, through a reconstructed text in which the fatal event is either accounted for or erased, undone.[13] In any event, this "stripped and free" feeling—a feeling of losing (also in the sense of loosing, dispersing) his life into another dimension—is what fascinates him in the spare, "spartan order" he thinks he sees in the lives of Leon, Emily and their child, at whose birth he had assisted as attending physician, effectively however fraudulently, before disappearing into the crowd.

Not thinking to disrupt that imagined order, only to enter it and thus to save himself from drowning in the medium of inescapable, self-perpetuating human entanglements, Morgan gradually finds in Emily what she, with silent calm contrapuntally opposed to his constant turmoil, finds in him:

> . . . once, passing a bookstore, Emily happened to notice a blown-up photo of the first successful powered flight, and the sight of Wilbur Wright poised on the sand at Kitty Hawk—capped and suited, strangely stylish, suspended forever in that tense, elated, ready position—reminded her for some reason of Morgan. (*MP* 212)

For all we know, Morgan has precisely such a cap and such a suit, some-where in his burgeoning closets . . . just on the chance . . . just as all his other impersonations—among them a traffic cop and a postman in addition to the uncertified physician, even a priest or a professor of sorts (to say nothing of his ostensibly "legitimate" job as a hardware-store manager)—turn out to have their essential truth, embedded within their flagrant falsity.

In a scene somehow the counterpart to that in which Emily sees Morgan in the image of Wilbur Wright, Morgan happens one day to see Emily, as if in a painting he is contemplating as a work finished and framed by another artist, yet also as if in a picture he is still in the process of composing himself, running (as she has lately begun to do) in the nearby streets:

> . . . and around the corner came Emily: a little black butterfly of a person with yellow feet [she is wearing yellow running shoes], far away. There was something about her running that seemed eternal. She was like the braided peasant girl in a weatherhouse, travelling forever on her appointed path, rain or shine, endearingly steadfast. Morgan felt himself grow weightless with happiness, and he expanded in the sunlight and beamed at everything with equal love: at Leon and the spindly, striving trees and Emily jogging up and away and the seagull wheeling overhead, floating though the chimneys in a languid search for the harbor. (*MP* 230–31)

Earthbound, Morgan and Emily jointly manifest at the end of the novel, as indeed each independently exhibits at the outset, "the obstinate en-durance of the human spirit, reflected in every character's acceptance or rejection of his fate" (in the terms of one characterization of her recurring subject as a novelist).[14] "Acceptance or rejection," in relation to "fate," has much the same ring as Paley's "real or invented" in relation to "destiny," not least in that both phrases contain seemingly alternative actions or conditions which are in fact bound together, each requiring to be enacted or endured in terms of the other. In their real *and* invented readiness to fly, more than in their power to remain aloft, Emily and Morgan pass the bounds of their own being. In surpassing they also resubmit to these shift-ing limits, which yet are constant in their continual redelineation. In reject-ing, they accept and recreate their separate and mutual fates, free and unfree of themselves as of the world, "the open destiny of life" in Tyler's view at once an affirmation and a contradiction in terms.

Real damage is done to those they leave behind—Emily's husband Leon, and especially Morgan's wife Bonny—even if in Tyler's world we are all complicit in the endgames of our failing relationships, even as we go on to create for ourselves the narrative accounts, and the moral or emotional accountings, in terms of which we survive. "We tell ourselves stories in order to live," writes Joan Didion.[15] After such knowledge, what for-giveness? For such woundings (or the guilt of those who inflict them) there is no redress in Tyler's fiction, forgiveness and unforgivability somehow alloyed in pain, and in the "slant" humor—containing a sense of "Zero at the Bone"—through which her characters' pain is characteristically expressed. Such pain is a medium of our humanity, but it is also both cause and effect of the ruthlessness of art, compassion residing in and inseparable from the coolness of Tyler's observing eye,[16] Morgan's selfishness and his selflessness one and the same.

In the words of the brother of Cher's intended in the movie "Moonstruck"—a romantic comedy which from time to time approaches the realistic "edge" of Tyler's comic romance—"Love 'roons' everything" (*roons*, he says—it wouldn't be the same without the Brooklyn accent), this lament then becoming a constructive argument in favor of proceeding with love's destructive course. In *Morgan's Passing* too, "love 'roons' everything," with "unsettling consequences for everyone," consequences most often charged to Morgan's overdrawn account. The seismic energy of such decompositions, however, also flows through the shifting fault planes of identity and behavior into *re*compositions of experience, in Morgan's mind but in the "real or invented" world as well, Morgan an expression of the world's inexhaustible self-artistry, as well as a consummate artist-of-the-self.[17]

As for Emily, it might as well have been Anne Tyler speaking, with equal parts of genial bemusement and a cool cordiality of representational control—perhaps to the reviewers of *Morgan's Passing* mentioned earlier, critics not wrong but slightly astray—when Emily has the following exchange with a mother for whose child's birthday party a puppet-show of "Beauty and the Beast" has just been performed; the woman pleased and yet perplexed, something not quite right:

> "Just one thing puzzles me," said Mrs. Tibbett.
> "What's that?"
> "Well, the Beast. He never changed to a prince."
> Leon glanced over at Emily.
> "Prince?" Emily said.
> "You had her living happily every after with the Beast. But *that's* not how it is; he changes; she says she loves him and he changes to a prince."
> "Oh," Emily said. It all came back to her now. She couldn't think how she'd forgotten. "Well . . ." she said.
> "But I guess that would take too many puppets."
> "No," Emily said, "it's just that we use a more authentic version."
> "Oh, I see," Mrs. Tibbett said. (*MP* 82–83)

She may not, but surely we do.

NOTES

["Morgan's Passion" was first prepared for presentation as a paper at the South Central Modern Language Association, Arlington, Texas, October, 1988, and, somewhat revised, at the Anne Tyler Symposium, Baltimore, April, 1989. I had earlier been asked to discuss *Morgan's Passing* with a public-library audience in Bartlesville, Oklahoma. I wish to thank Mary Alice O'Toole, who invited me to Bartlesville, James G. Watson, who chaired the "American Literature since 1900" section at SCMLA, and, particularly, C. Ralph Stephens, who directed the Anne Tyler Symposium, for these opportunities to speak, which led to the opportunity to contribute an essay to this volume, now further revised but still written in the spirit of the original talks.]

1. Robert Towers, *The New Republic*, 182 (22 March 1980), 28.

2. "The Art of Fiction," *Henry James, Literary Criticism: Essays on Literature, American Writers, English Writers*, selected and annotated by Leon Edel (New York: The Library of America, 1984), p. 55.

3. *them* (New York: Vanguard, 1969), p. 224.

4. In *Enormous Changes at the Last Minute* (New York: Farrar Straus Giroux, 1974), p. 162.

5. "Imagining Things," *The New Yorker*, 56 (23 June 1980), 97.

6. Quoted in *Contemporary Authors: New Revision Series,* vol. 11, ed. Ann Evory and Linda Metzger (Detroit: Gale Research, 1984), p. 510.

7. "About Maggie, Who Tried Too Hard," *The New York Times Book Review*, 11 September 1988, p. 1.

8. "Two Novels," *The New York Times Book Review,* 28 April 1974, p. 34.

9. Katha Politt says of Tyler's novels, "They are modern in their fictional techniques, yet utterly unconcerned with the contemporary moment as a subject, so that, with only minor dislocations, her stories could just as well have taken place in the twenties or thirties" (*The New York Times Book Review,* 18 January 1976, p. 22).

10. Quoted by Bruce Cook in "New Faces in Faulkner Country," *The Saturday Review,* 59 (4 September 1976), 40.

11. Quoted in *Contemporary Authors* (see n. 6 above), p. 511.

12. In *Final Harvest: Emily Dickinson's Poems,* ed. Thomas H. Johnson (Boston: Little Brown, 1962), p. 228.

13. A. G. Mojtaba, reviewing *Morgan's Passing* in *The New York Times Book Review* (23 March 1980, p. 33), said, "This might have been the story of a midlife crisis, a familiar tale, with steady, reliable associations, however tormented; but Miss Tyler chose instead to depict an unfamiliar state of continual crisis, a condition for which there exist no charts or manuals ready to hand."

14. Mary Ellen Brooks, "Anne Tyler," *Dictionary of Literary Biography*, vol. 6: *American Novelists Since World War II, Second Series,* ed. James E. Kibler, Jr. (Detroit: Gale Research, 1980), p. 337.

15. *The White Album* (New York: Simon and Schuster, 1979), p. 11.

16. During the Anne Tyler Symposium in Baltimore in April, 1989, Joseph C. Voelker stated, in response to remarks about the nature of the novelist's "sympathy" for her characters, that Tyler "casts a cold eye" on the situations of those she portrays. He did so in terms at once invoking, and inquiring into the usefulness of, a comparison of Tyler with Mary McCarthy. But he also suggested—McCarthy or any other writer aside—that Tyler's "compassion" for her characters (of which much was made at the meeting) should be seen in the context of a certain impassivity, even pitilessness, of artistic detachment, perhaps rooted less in a theory of art than in a personal sense of the inexorabilities of life.

17. In *Morgan's Passing,* John Leonard wrote in *The New York Times* (17 March 1980, sec. C, p. 17), Tyler "is asking whether art is adequate to the impersonations life insists on, death absolves."

Beck Tull: "The absent presence" in *Dinner at the Homesick Restaurant*

JOSEPH B. WAGNER

Beck would not have known them. And they, perhaps, would not have known Beck. They never asked about him. Didn't that show how little importance a father has? The invisible man. The absent presence. Pearl felt a twinge of angry joy. Apparently she had carried this off— made the transition so smoothly that not a single person guessed. It was the greatest triumph of her life. (DHR 20)

With this elaborate meditation, Pearl Tull tries to deny the agonizing humiliation she has felt since her husband announced that he doesn't "want to stay married" (*DHR* 9) and that he "won't be visiting the children" (*DHR* 10). Pearl's response is at once puzzled and cogent: "I don't understand you." In fact, she never does understand, and he never provides an explanation; thus, she cannot talk to her children about their loss, and they must discover for themselves that their father has left them.

Naturally, the children never understand, either—not, at least, until the last scene in the book when Cody is reminded of the time he and Ezra squabbled over an archery set, accidentally wounding their mother with an arrow. Beck has finally returned, and he is trying to explain to Cody the prevailing sense of defeat that drove him away:

> No matter how hard I tried, seemed like everything I did got muddled. Spoiled. Turned into an accident. . . . Do you recall the archery set? I thought it would be such fun, set up a target on a tree trunk and shoot our bows and arrows. . . . Then you and Ezra get in some kind of, I don't know, argument or quarrel, end up scuffling, shoot off an arrow, and wing your mother. . . . Shot her through the shoulder. A disaster, a typical disaster. Then something goes wrong with the wound. Something, I don't know, some infection or other. For me, it was the very last straw. I was sitting over a beer in the kitchen that Sunday evening and all at once, not even knowing I'd do it, I said, "Pearl, I'm leaving." (*DHR* 300–01)

As this incident is what finally defeats Beck, it becomes the book's most critical event, and (except for Pearl herself) the absence which results is the single most powerful factor in the development of the central characters. Cody, Ezra, and Jenny are, respectively, 14, 11, and 9 years old when Beck leaves. The rest of their lives are so molded by that departure that their personalities correspond to psychoanalytic profiles of children who, at similar ages, are also abandoned by their fathers.

When the archery accident occurs, Beck is capitulating in an overt struggle with his oldest son. As we know from Pearl's account of the accident, she was wounded—indeed, pierced—"through the heart; or not the heart exactly, but the fleshy part above it, between breast and shoulder" (*DHR* 28). We also know that the arrow was Cody's, that it was tauntingly aimed at Ezra, that Ezra had helped create the catastrophe by trying to prevent it, and that ultimately each of the three males carried his own share of blame for the incident. The piercing of the mother by the son's wayward arrow is not only an elaborate vignette that Tyler employs in bringing about the departure of the father. It provides the controlling metaphor for his oedipal defeat. The permanence of his loss later becomes evident when he tells Cody of the time he tried to return home and had stood outside the house, timidly waiting for someone to appear: "I guess I was going to introduce myself or something, if anybody came out" (*DHR* 301). But the person who did appear was not one who would welcome him, or tell him he was needed. It was the same son who had unwittingly vanquished him, and who now appeared even more formidable to the absent father:

> It was you that came. First I didn't even know you, wondered if someone else had moved in. Then I realized it was just that you had grown so. You were almost a man. You came down the walk and you bent for the evening paper and as you straightened, you kind of flipped it in the air and caught it again, and I saw that you could live without me. (*DHR* 301–02)

In a sense, someone else *had* moved in. As Beck saw it, another man—his own son, Cody—had taken his place, even though Cody certainly did not aspire to such a role. In fact, Cody and his brother and sister grow up yearning for their father. Their behavior illustrates what psychoanalysts call "father hunger":

> Children without fathers experience father hunger, an affective state of considerable tenacity and force. Father hunger appears to be a critical motivational variable in matters as diverse as caretaking, sexual orientation, moral development, and achievement level. . . . [Such] children feel . . . they lack something that they vitally need. . . . The ambivalence, hurt, and hatred . . . seem to maximize for the child the felt absence of a masculine parent and to exacerbate father hunger. . . .[1]

In some cases, the ramifications of such loss include extreme anger and hostility, but if the mother has effectively dominated a boy, he "may have difficulty in valuing and identifying with the male role . . ." and he also may establish "a prolonged symbiotic tie"[2] with his mother. The hostile Cody and the passive Ezra can readily illustrate such diametrically opposite personalities. For Cody, all of life is angry competition, perhaps best illustrated in the "long and arduous battle campaign" that he'd launched to steal Ruth from "Ezra, his oldest enemy" (*DHR* 151–52). By contrast, when the middle-aged Ezra is left alone to nurse his blind and frail mother, he realizes that "he had trusted his mother to be everything for him," and he still wonders, "how could he depend on such a person? Why had she let him down so?" (*DHR* 261)

So far as Jenny is concerned, Lora Heims Tessman's "A Note on the Father's Contribution to the Daughter's Ways of Loving and Working" can be helpful. It observes that a young girl will frequently react to her father's departure with "a sense of rejection of her erotic feelings [which] may become . . . an area of lifelong vulnerability, associated with various defensive reactions" and an inability to realize "opportunities for further affectionate interaction."[3] Additionally, "if he praises her skills, but keeps himself greatly distant, her achievements may feel barren to her, as though the essence of herself has been rejected."[4]

Juxtaposing such descriptions with the children of the Tull family indicates that, among other things, they provide us with psychologically credible profiles of children suffering from "father hunger." Tyler carefully develops Cody's aggression, Jenny's detachment, and Ezra's passivity as haunting effects of Beck's absence. Further, although Pearl is unable to understand Beck's reasons for leaving or to acknowledge its impact on her children, she does see that each of them has developed a serious deficiency. She worries that:

> Something was wrong with all of her children. . . . She sensed a kind of trademark flaw in each of their lives. Cody was prone to unreasonable rages; Jenny was so flippant; Ezra hadn't really lived up to his potential. . . . She wondered if her children blamed her for something. . . . (*DHR* 22)

Pearl is right: there *is* something wrong with her children, and each of them knows it, at least in part. In his or her own way, each carries an emptiness, an absence, to correspond to the hunger caused by the deprivation of a father. Jenny, for instance, who "claimed to have forgotten all about" (*DHR* 285) her father, is unable to achieve intimacy in any of her three marriages. Her first marriage (to Harley Baines) is pathetic in its uninspired orderliness; her second (to Sam Wiley) requires too much passion; and her third (to Joe St. Ambrose and his large family) merely provides the necessary shelter of chaos. That is, since she must now care for six children, Jenny has no choice but to treat them with the same mixture of detached concern and amused irony that she has for the patients in her pediatrics practice. She approaches her life with a benign but distancing sense of humor that renders tolerable many burdens but also creates a defensive shell penetrable by no one. As a result of this insularity, Jenny will never accept the central, focal role in someone else's life, nor will she allow another to play such a crucial part in hers. Indeed, soon after her second marriage (and her only intense love affair) disintegrates, Jenny has to struggle mightily to maintain her mental balance, and we are given a detailed picture of the way in which she builds a fortification of emotional distance around herself:

> She would remind herself to draw back, to loosen hold. It seemed to her that the people she admired . . . had this in common: they gazed at the world from a distance. . . . She was learning how to make it through life on a slant. She was trying to lose her intensity. . . . Then she met Joe with his flanks of children—his padding, his moat, his barricade of children, all in urgent need of her brisk and competent attention. No conversation *there*—she and Joe had hardly found a moment to speak to each other seriously. (*DHR* 212–13)

Sadly, Joe would like to speak to Jenny seriously, as we learn when he tries to discuss the idea of having more children. In the midst of preparing dinner for all the children they already have, Jenny innocently trivializes the idea, but she also trivializes Joe's awkward attempt at having an intimate conversation:

> Joe said if they did have a baby, he'd like it to be a girl. He'd looked around and noticed they were a little short on girls. "How can you say that?" Jenny asked. She ticked the girls off on her fingers: "Phoebe, Becky, Jane . . . "
> * * * *
> "That's only three."
> She felt a little rush of confusion. "Have I left one out?"
> * * * *
> "I'm trying to have a conversation here."
> "Isn't that what we're doing?"
> "Yes, yes . . . "
> "Then where's the problem?" (*DHR* 200)

After several silent minutes of Joe's "scowling" and Jenny's being "puzzled," "Jenny laughed, and Joe glared at her and wheeled and stamped out of the kitchen" (*DHR* 201).

Jenny is efficient and competent, but she learns that she cannot love intimately. In that realm, "she saw that she had always been doomed to fail, had been unlovable, had lacked some singular quality that would keep a husband. She had never known this consciously" until she was eight months' pregnant and the marriage with Sam Wiley was almost over, "but the pain she felt was eerily familiar—like a suspicion, long held, at last confirmed" (*DHR* 208). Jenny is a good example of the daughters who react to their fathers' early departure with "a sense of rejection," who manifest "a lifelong vulnerability," and who have great difficulties in finding "opportunities for further affectionate interaction."[5]

Perhaps it is not a coincidence that Jenny is the one family member who, though present, is not involved in the accident with the bow and arrow. Although the occasion was clearly a family outing and although the longest account of the incident (*DHR* 35–39) carefully details the appearance and behavior of the other family members, it contains just two brief references to Jenny, and they serve to underscore the peripheral nature of her role: she "buttoned her sweater with chapped and bluish hands" (*DHR* 36), and when Ezra's good luck brings him a bull's eye, she is seen "running to get [to the target] first" (*DHR* 38). In other words, she is isolated by her fragility until the time comes for her to celebrate and cheer her brother's feat. Throughout the scene, Jenny does not participate at all in the important dynamics of the others' strained relationships, and she is peculiarly absent from the narrative of the actual shooting and its aftermath. So Jenny is marginalized in the symbolically crucial scene of the Tull family's power struggle, just as she continues to feel marginalized through her later life.

Like his sister, Ezra, too, doesn't seem to care about Beck, but unlike his sister, he does not try to deceive himself. He realizes "that it . . . was true: he really didn't care" (*DHR* 284). In spite of his warmth and generosity, Ezra is very much a lethargic and empty person: he sees himself as "defenseless; and he'd felt defenseless as a child, too, he believed" (*DHR* 261). Ezra recognizes and regrets his own passivity, but he feels helpless in changing it and reflects that:

> he had never married, never fathered children, and lost the one girl he had loved out of sheer fatalism, lack of force, a willing assumption of defeat. (*Let it be* was the theme that ran through his life. He was ruled by a dreamy mood of acceptance that was partly the source of all his happiness and partly his undoing.) (*DHR* 266)

Like his restaurant, Ezra is completely open, simplified to the point of being hollowed out and, as he puts it, "defenseless." His "dreamy . . . acceptance," especially when he surrenders "the one girl he had loved" to his brother, is so extreme that it can lead to speculation on the nature of his sexuality. The absence of a boy's father may cause "fear" of "assuming a male role" because that "may mean being devalued, dominated, and belittled by mother; thus in doing so he risks his esteemed relationship with her, a relationship that may be based on a prolonged symbiotic tie."[6] In his essay on "The Sexual Aberrations" Freud considers parental presence to be an important "accidental factor" in deciding "a person's final sexual attitude":

> A person's final sexual attitude is not decided until after puberty and is the result of a number of factors. . . . We have observed that the presence of both parents plays an important part. The absence of a strong father in childhood not infrequently favours the occurrence of inversion.[7]

Freud's view on this point is generally confirmed by the work of later analysts. For instance, C.W. Socarides describes the usual family constellation of the male homosexual: "a domineering, psychologically crushing mother and an absent, weak, hostile, or rejecting father."[8] In the same essay, Socarides explains that "it is the father's love that helps diminish the child's fear of loss of the mother's love. . . . If the child does not have the father to turn to, he experiences a severe deflation of his developing sense of self-esteem . . . and the painful realization of his own helplessness."[9] In his own classic work, *The Overt Homosexual* (1968), Socarides writes that "the absence of the father or the presence of a weak father combined with a domineering, harsh and phallic mother favors the development of homosexuality."[10]

All of this is not to say that Ezra is homosexual (that point would be nearly irrelevant to the discreetly private sexuality of Tyler's characters, in any event) but that his early "family constellation" of absent father and domineering mother may have weakened his ability to determine his sexual identity and encouraged him first to pursue his happiness only hesitantly and then to relinquish Ruth quietly and with puzzlement, saying only that "I'm sure I'll understand in a minute" (*DHR* 163). It is surely true that the Tull household was not only marked by an absent father but by "a domineering, harsh," even tyrannical mother as well. It is also true that Ezra reacted to her in his characteristically mild way.[11]

It should be remembered that, despite their interest in him, Ezra never pays particular attention to women until the noticeably boyish Ruth enters his life, and with her he establishes a symbiotic friendship more than a love affair. Unlike Cody, who indulges in erotic fantasies about Ruth, Ezra establishes a nearly platonic courtship with her. There is a tender familiarity between them, but they are comrades more than lovers. A scene in which they are walking home from the restaurant is typical:

> Ezra had his pearwood recorder. He played it as he walked, serious and absorbed, with his lashes lowered on his cheeks. "Le Godiveau de Poisson," he

78

played. Passersby looked at him and smiled. Ruth hummed along with some notes, fell into her own thoughts at others. Then Ezra put his recorder in the pocket of his shabby lumber jacket, and he and Ruth began discussing the menu. It was good they were serving the rice dish, Ruth said; that always made the Arab family happy. She ran her fingers through her sprouty red hair. Cody, walking on the other side of her, felt her shift of weight when Ezra circled her with one arm and pulled her close. (*DHR* 143–44)

Ezra is comfortable and reliable in his love, but it cannot be coincidental that the only people to elicit strong emotional reactions from him are the sad misfit Josiah, the surrogate mother Mrs. Scarlatti, and the surrogate son Luke.

Ezra, of course, was centrally involved in the crucial archery accident that Tyler eventually re-tells from the various perspectives of all the participants. It was Ezra who panicked and "ran toward him [Cody], flapping his arms like an idiot and stammering, 'Stop, stop, stop! No! Stop!' [He] took a flying leap with his arms outstretched like a lover. He caught Cody in a kind of bear hug and slammed him flat on his back. . . . And meanwhile, what had happened to the arrow?"(*DHR* 39) Pearl was "hobbling in his direction with a perfect circle of blood gleaming on the shoulder of her blouse." With typical anger and solipsism, Cody blames only his brother: "'See there?' Cody asked him. 'See what you've gone and done?' 'Did *I* do that?' 'Gone and done it to me again,' Cody said, and he staggered to his feet and walked away." (*DHR* 39) The force of the accusation stays with Ezra forever: his brother does not particularly remember the incident again until he is reminded of it at the end of the book, but Ezra remembers: "'I'm so sorry, I'm sorry, I'm sorry,' he had cried, but the apology had never been accepted because his brother had been blamed instead, and his father, who had purchased the archery set. Ezra, his mother's favorite, had got off scot-free. He'd been left unforgiven—not relieved, as you might expect, but forever burdened." (*DHR* 120)

Poor Ezra: the unforgiven, forever burdened, incomplete man. One of many questions about this book is why Ezra seems to be both central and peripheral. For instance, the title of the book and the focal point of its setting are clearly Ezra's—they invoke a sense of his place, his restaurant. Also, he is easily the most admired and probably the most loved character in the book's family. And he is the one family member who provides care for his mother when she is dying. So it is necessary that for the final dinner, Ezra be the one to call the family together at his home and his restaurant. But the real reunion with Beck is given to Cody. It is Cody who finds his father, who sits with him on the sidewalk and who learns why he had left thirty-five years earlier, and (most interestingly) it is Cody who, in the book's final paragraph, is at last able to perform a generous deed:

Cody held on to his [Beck's] elbow and led him toward the others. Overhead, seagulls drifted through a sky so clear and blue that it brought back all the outings of his boyhood—the drives, the picnics, the autumn hikes, the wild-flower walks in the spring. He remembered the archery trip, and it seemed to him now that he even remembered that arrow sailing in its graceful, fluttering path. He remembered his mother's upright form along the grasses, her hair lit gold, her small hands smoothing her bouquet while the arrow journeyed on. And high above, he seemed to recall, there had been a little brown airplane, almost motionless, droning through the sunshine like a bumblebee. (*DHR* 303)

For once, Cody's memory is not harshly accurate; now it is delicate, *albeit* unreliable. What he had earlier seen as the sustained ugliness of their lives is now gone. Cody is uncharacteristically gentle and at peace with himself, his memories have shifted from deprivation to fulfillment, his mother's sharpness is finally softened, and even the arrow is transformed from bru-tality to grace. Why should Cody be so privileged by this nirvana-like rev-erie? It would seem that Ezra ought to be given the restorative and generous work of welcoming the prodigal father. Surely, a reader might wish that Ezra be given the blessing of the "little brown airplane."

But Cody is the only right choice because though Ezra may deserve a blessing, Cody needs one, and so does his father. The father and the oldest son are the primary players in the central oedipal struggle which shapes all the other relationships in the book. It was Cody who had refused to ac-quiesce and to heed his father's instructions on how to shoot his arrow. In fact, in that early scene, Cody reflected on his father's contemptible inade-quacy: "He looked like a fool, Cody thought" (*DHR* 35). We also know that when Beck began to bully Cody, he retaliated by maliciously aiming the arrow at Ezra before he mistakenly released it.

Of the three children, Cody was most twisted by his father's departure and is the primary cause of his mother's worry:

Cody, in particular, referred continually to Pearl's short temper. . . . Hon-estly, she thought, wasn't there some statute of limitations here? When was he going to absolve her? He was middle-aged. He had no business holding her responsible any more. (*DHR* 22–23)

Cody almost perfectly embodies John Munder Ross' observations about the anger that some boys feel in response to unloving or absent fathers:

If the father seems remote, hostile, or authoritarian, his son may well seize on sex as an altogether sadistic act more or less isolated from familial love, and may contrive for himself a variety of violent fantasies about it. As with the mother of infancy, parental absences incite rage, which is projected, coloring the child's image of the missing father.[12]

Cody's hostility is unmitigated and, except in his dreams, he displays no vulnerability; until the final scene of the book, there is not a single instance of compassion or kindness in all of his activity. He is regularly surly and contemptuous of those who are around him, and especially of those who love him. In addition, it is only Cody who has done things that are surely evil: stealing Ruth from Ezra and denying his son Luke by absurdly insisting that he is Ezra's and not his own (*DHR* 226). So it is Cody's conflicts which, above all, must be resolved. The stories of the other family members may be heart-wrenching, but they are not at the heart of the matter.

Tyler specifically connects the centrality of Cody's unresolved oedipal hostility to his father's absence. Just a few months after Beck's departure, there is a scene in which Cody finds his mother in her bedroom and asks, "When is Dad coming home?" Pearl evades the question with "Oh, pretty soon," and Cody looks about, reflecting on the spartan, lifeless quality of his home. He asks himself, "Who wouldn't leave such a place?" But at that most inopportune moment, his mother smiles at him, comes over to him, smooths his hair, and says:

> "My . . . you're getting so big! I can't believe it."
> He shrank back in his seat.
> "You're getting big enough for me to start relying on," she said.
> "I'm only fourteen," Cody told her. (*DHR* 42)

He leaves the room immediately and resorts to an immature prank, emphasizing that he is indeed an adolescent who is neither willing nor able to serve as his father's surrogate: he walks past the bathroom, hears Ezra singing in the shower, and goes through the house turning on every hot water faucet—very much in pursuit of a boy's business, not a man's.

If Cody had been younger, Pearl might have succeeded in recruiting him for her surrogate husband (as she eventually did do in the case of Ezra, who spent his life as her companion), and she might have compromised his hostile and conquering sexuality. But this does not happen to Pearl and Cody. In reality, she only deepens his hostility. Cody was badly hurt and frightened by his father's departure, but he cannot share his trouble with anyone. He suffers from guilt-ridden dreams (*DHR* 47), and in his conscious musings he resents his father, who had "uprooted the family continually" and then left them, "had ruined their lives . . . first in one way and then in another" (*DHR* 59). He saw Beck's departure quite specifically as abandoning the children into the hands of their very destructive mother. At the end of the book, Beck reacts to news of Cody's financial success by blandly exclaiming, "Is that so. Well, I sure am proud of you, son." Cody can only wonder, "Was that all he had been striving for—this one brief moment of respect flitting across his father's face?" (*DHR* 291) He accuses Beck: "You left us in her clutches"; and he demands to know, "How could you do that?" "How could you just dump us on our mother's mercy?" (*DHR* 299–300)

In his discussion of the developing sexual identity in adolescents, Aaron H. Esman may have someone like Cody in mind when he describes "the early adolescent boy" who "is suddenly deprived of his primary role model":

> The absence of the father may confront him with the anxieties attendant on an imagined oedipal triumph on the one hand, and a regressively tinged intensity of intimacy on the other. Both may be aggravated when the mother seeks unconsciously to use her son as a replacement for her lost husband.[13]

This is exactly what happens to Cody when his mother suggests that he be his father's surrogate, but he cannot even begin to understand until that final scene, when he takes his wayward father's elbow and leads him back "toward the others" (*DHR* 303). For the first time he remembers his childhood with pleasure rather than bitterness, and he responds to his family with gentleness rather than anger. Cody and his father are appropriately alone in this scene: only these two need the blessing and the forgiveness symbolized by the book's final image, that cruciform airplane in Cody's memory that is still "droning through the sunshine like a bumblebee."

Pearl had asked when Cody would "absolve her" (*DHR* 23) of the responsibility for his unhappiness, but she does not need absolution in the way that Cody and Beck do. In spite of her flaws, Pearl labored to hold her family together; Cody and Beck worked to deny and dissolve their family. Thus, only they have committed wrongs that require forgiveness, and if others had been present when Cody finally recalls the airplane, its significance as a sign of absolution would be diluted. Perhaps the ultimate irony is that the "absent presence" which will now hover over the lives of the Tull family is not Beck's, but Pearl's.

NOTES

1. James M. Herzog, "On Father Hunger: The Father's Role in the Modulation of Aggressive Drive and Fantasy," in *Father and Child: Developmental and Clinical Perspectives*, ed. Stanley H. Cath, et al. (Boston: Little, Brown, 1982), p. 174.

2. Phyllis Tyson, "The Role of the Father in Gender Identity, Urethral Erotism, and Phallic Narcissism," in *Father and Child*, pp. 183–84.

3. In *Father and Child*, p. 222.

4. Ibid., p. 227.

5. Ibid., p. 222.

6. Tyson, pp. 183–84.

7. Sigmund Freud, "Three Essays on the Theory of Sexuality" (1905) in *The Standard Edition of the Complete Psychological Works of Sigmund Freud*, VII, ed. James Strachey (London: Hogarth Press, 1953), pp. 145–46.

8. "Abdicating Fathers, Homosexual Sons: Psychoanalytic Observations on the

Contribution of the Father to the Development of Male Homosexuality," in *Father and Child*, p. 509.

9. Ibid., p. 514.

10. (New York: Grune & Stratton), p. 84.

11. Once, for example, when "their mother went on one of her rampages" (*DHR* 49), Ezra responded by saying:

> "I wish we could just go off . . . and not come back till it's over."
> "It won't be over till she's had her scene," Cody told him. "You know that. There's no way we can get around it."
> "I wish Daddy were here."
> "Well, he's not, so shut up." (*DHR* 50)

Several minutes later, while at the supper table, Cody confronts Pearl with the injustice of her "rampage," and the reaction that Tyler describes is a masterful evocation of maternal anxiety turned into rage:

> Pearl threw the spoon in his face. "You upstart," she said. She rose and slapped him across the cheek. "You wretch, you ugly horror." She grabbed one of Jenny's braids and yanked it so Jenny was pulled off her chair. "Stupid clod," she said to Ezra, and she took the bowl of peas and brought it down on his head. It didn't break, but peas flew everywhere. Ezra cowered, shielding his head with his arms. "Parasites," she told them. "I wish you'd all die, and let me go free. I wish I'd find you dead in your beds." (*DHR* 53)

12. "From Mother to Father: The Boy's Search for a Generative Identity and the Oedipal Era," in *Father and Child*, pp. 199–200.

13. "Fathers and Adolescent Sons," in *Father and Child*, p. 272.

Traveling Towards the Self: The Psychic Drama of Anne Tyler's *The Accidental Tourist*

ANNE RICKETSON ZAHLAN

A nne Tyler makes new the perennial American struggle with the conflicting claims of stability and freedom, the contrary urges to settle and to roam. Her characters speculate about changing places and switching families, and her novels abound with departures and returns. Tyler herself, she tells us in "Still Just Writing," is continually prepared to travel. "It is physically impossible for me," she confesses, "to buy any necessity without buying a travel-sized version as well. I have a little toilet kit, with soap and a nightgown, forever packed and ready to go."[1] Paralleling journey in space with journey in time, Tyler's fiction counterpoises the tendency to accumulate people and things with the urge to travel and to travel light. Possessed by desire and anxiety, determined to live free, Tyler's wanderers resist society's repressive attempts to box them in and lock them up: "How come," wonders Jake Simms, "this world has so many ways of tying a person down?" (*EP* 95)

Bank robber, jail-bird, hostage-taker, and demolition specialist, Jake Simms of *Earthly Possessions* is perhaps the most rebellious of Tyler's fictional travelers. He is not, however, the only one. Beck Tull in *Dinner at the Homesick Restaurant*, Morgan Gower in *Morgan's Passing*, and Caleb Peck and his great-nephew Duncan in *Searching for Caleb* all flee responsibility in pursuit of liberty. Charlotte Emory of *Earthly Possessions*, hostage to Jake Simms, is compelled to make the journey she had longed to take to

84

escape the demands of marriage and family and the accumulated clutter of a lifetime spent in one house. "My life," Charlotte claims, "has been a history of casting off encumbrances, paring down to the bare essentials, stripping for the journey" (*EP* 37).

As the narrative of *Earthly Possessions* lays out the warring impulses with all but absolute symmetry, *Searching for Caleb* works towards fusion. The story of a quest for a lost brother, *Searching for Caleb* pits the values of property and tribal allegiance against the charms of getting away. It also paradoxically attests to a possible coexistence between binding ties and traveling light. Justine and Duncan Peck live life on the move, but Justine's devotion to her wanderer-husband does not prevent her alliance with Grandfather Peck, who has joined the vagabond household without relinquishing one whit of his Peck rigidity. As Justine and her grandfather travel together in ostensible search of the defector Caleb, the journey becomes an effort to reconstitute both family and self, a means to fuse gathering in and moving on.

Even more than in Tyler's other fiction, the motif of travel organizes *The Accidental Tourist*. The novel's protagonist, Macon Leary (like his creator devoted to travel-sized toiletries), journeys by car and cab, by train, and on planes, large and small. He remains, however, a traveler who would prefer not to go. A man who dotes on appliance maintenance contracts and makes no purchase without consulting *Consumer Reports,* Tyler's Macon keeps a file of detailed written directions without which he would go hopelessly astray in the city of his birth. This "geographic dyslexia" (*AT* 116), a Leary family trait, renders Macon peculiarly unfit for journeying. He is ill-prepared to travel, not just over the lands and seas of the external world, but also in life's journey through time and the prerequisite exploration of the self.

In *The Accidental Tourist,* Tyler explores in psychic terms the tension between the impulse to roam and the urge to stay put. Born into the "cautious half" of humanity, Macon Leary must deal with the inner conflict between demanding id and legislating superego. Despite the inciting tragedy, the plot is comic and the conflict is resolved. And both conflict and eventual resolution find a figure in the logo that replaces signature on Macon's guidebooks for travelers whose "concern was how to pretend they had never left home" (*AT* 12). Offering sour advice on "Trying to Eat . . . " or "Trying to Sleep . . . " in England or wherever, the books are the work of a man who insulates himself from his fellow-travelers with carefully constructed barricades of piled-up luggage and a forbidding thousand-page novel. He avoids all contact with those others who inhabit the cities he visits; he is the most reluctant of tourists:

> Macon hated travel. He careened through foreign countries on a desperate kind of blitz—squinching his eyes shut and holding his breath and hanging on for dear life, he sometimes imagined—and then settled back home with a

sigh of relief to produce his chunky passport-sized paperbacks. *Accidental Tourist in France. Accidental Tourist in Germany. In Belgium.* (*AT* 12)

The guidebooks are anonymous: "No author's name, just a logo: a winged armchair on the cover" (*AT* 12). And the signature armchair is overstuffed and welcoming, a seductive image of the inertias of home. It is also provided with the wings of movement, of travel, of flight. "While armchair travelers dream of going places," Macon's publisher explains, "traveling armchairs dream of staying put" (*AT* 89).

As much as Macon "hated the travel, he loved the writing—the virtuous delights of organizing a disorganized country" (*AT* 12). "Stripping away the inessential . . . [and] classifying all that remained in neat, terse paragraphs" (*AT* 12), Macon turns out books dedicated to eradicating foreignness. As historians impose ideological structure on the raw material of chronicle and document—as, in fact, human beings create their lives through psychic narrative—so Macon manipulates the experience of travel to create a self he thinks he wants to be. In Tyler's *The Accidental Tourist,* Macon Leary, leary of life, cannot confront the experience of a lost son and a failed marriage. Reluctant to try to shape a self capable of negotiating life, unwilling to overcome the psychic version of his geographic dyslexia, Macon is incapable of salutary narrative. His tersely phrased and punctiliously punctuated works consist wholly of the life-denying evasions of "the accidental tourist."

Although Macon's own narratives offer no hope of regeneration, Tyler's novel recounts a journey through psychic despair to rebirth. In *The Accidental Tourist,* the battle between the need for safety and the urge to adventure is fought out on psychic ground, within the single self. This inward displacement of tension is symbolically suggested by a third characteristic of the armchair logo—a matter of absence: the chair is empty and the struggle is for the self. As the wings are fused to the armchair, so are the conflicting desires to take shelter and to seek adventure compressed within the tormented psyche of Macon Leary.

Bereft of his murdered child as the novel begins, Macon is soon abandoned by his wife of twenty years. Alone and affectively dead, he is reduced to subsisting on popcorn and sleeping in shroud-like "body-bags" to save on laundry. Stooped and sloppy in a gray sweat-suit that he has taken to wearing night and day, Macon catches sight of himself in a mirror and recoils at the image: "His reflection reminded him of a patient in a mental hospital" (*AT* 56). Macon's moment of shocked misrecognition is the first of several mirror scenes in the novel. Its significance may be elucidated with reference to Jacques Lacan's notion of the mirror stage as the point at which the child perceiving the self as other and recognizing the self in the other begins to develop an "integrated self-image."[2] For Lacan such perception "projects the individual into history." Thus, "the *mirror stage* is a drama whose internal thrust is precipitated from insufficiency to anticipation": it "manufactures for the subject, caught up in . . . spatial identification, the succession of phantasies that extends from a fragmented body-image to a form of its totality that I shall call orthopaedic—and, lastly, to the assumption of the armor of an alienating identity."[3] As Charlotte in *Earthly Possessions* actively constructs a self through narrative episodes, so Macon's self is passively formed and transformed in a succession of reflected images. In this initial repetition of mirror-stage misrecognition, Macon glimpses his own disorder and is impelled towards the violent fall prerequisite to recovery.

Macon's "fortunate fall" is down the basement steps. Hoisted on the petard of his absurd energy-saving household system, he is knocked off balance by his justifiably resistant dog. The resulting broken leg liberates him from the loveless house of his dismantled family. Physical incapacity entitles him to take refuge in the family home, where his sister presides over a painstakingly alphabetized kitchen, and recreation consists of a family card-game so deliberately complicated that no outsider can penetrate the Byzantine intricacies of its "rules." Safely reunited in the house of their youth, the middle-aged Leary siblings ignore the telephone (messenger from the outside world) and eat their childhood-favorite baked potatoes: "there was something about the smell of a roasting Idaho that was so cozy, and also, well, *conservative,* was the way Macon put it to himself" (*AT* 77).

Perceiving his reflected self as a "mental patient," Macon is impelled to reenact a child's first psychic steps towards integration of self. Enclosed in an imaginary "dimension of images," his conscious self engaged in that misrecognition which could initiate self-perception.[4] Encased in the plaster cast that will help mend his fractured body, Macon has outwardly assumed what Lacan terms "the armor of an alienating identity": "He was sealed away from himself" (*AT* 60). At once crippled and insulated by plaster, Macon seeks refuge in the house where the Leary grandparents lived and died and to which, one by one, the Leary brothers return from their failed marriages, a domain of law and the super-ego. Aware of the comfort he finds in such protective structures, Macon is moved to wonder "whether by some devious, subconscious means, he had engineered this injury—every elaborate step leading up to it—just so he could settle down safe among the people he'd started out with" (*AT* 63).

The Leary house is the house not of the father, but of the grandfather; Macon's father died when his children were young, and remains throughout the novel not just absent but unnamed. The "name of the father" is thus replaced by the name of the grandfather, adding parodic emphasis to Freud's association of parental authority and the super-ego. "The role, which the super-ego undertakes later in life," Freud tells us, "is at first played by . . . parental authority."[5] Thus in retreating to the paternal, the doubly paternal domain, Tyler's Macon Leary seeks to reinstate the primary situation in which parental authority offered not just restriction but also security.[6] He thus attempts to evade—by unconditional surrender—the suffering imposed by the "harshness" of the super-ego.

The repressive Freudian super-ego is, in Lacanian thought, associated with the "symbolic order," a primarily verbal order described by Terry Eagleton as the "pre-given structure of social and sexual roles and relations which make up the family and society."[7] Thus when Macon seeks refuge in the Leary house, he moves from an imaginary register of images into the symbolic order.[8] Grandfather Leary, a paternal image at once removed and redoubled, exercised control through language, by appeals to the power of connotation. When a teen-aged Macon dated, he was chauffeured by his stern grandfather and relegated to the "velvety gray backseat" of a "long black Buick" where he sat irrevocably alone; the backseat, a shared backseat anyway, had, according to Grandfather Leary's decree, "'connotations.' (Much of Macon's youth was ruled by connotations)" (*AT* 50). Such verbal sensitivity underscores the relevance to Macon's world of the association predicated by Lacan between super-ego, family, law, and the register of language. "The primordial Law," Lacan points out, is "that which in reg-ulating marriage ties superimposes the kingdom of culture on that of a nature abandoned to the law of mating." The laws and prohibitions imposed upon marriage are therefore "identical with an order of language."[9] The Learys pay scrupulous attention to the order of language: they concern themselves with fine points of usage; they refer often to the dictionary. Macon's exasperated wife details the preoccupations of her Leary in-laws:

> Playing that ridiculous card game no one else can fathom. . . . Plotting your little household projects. . . . Cruising hardware stores like other people cruise boutiques. . . . Picking apart people's English. . . . Hauling forth the dictionary at every opportunity. Quibbling over *method*. . . . (*AT* 137–38)

Macon Leary fails in his attempt to take cowardly refuge in the censorship of the super-ego, and the obstacle to his escape is his constant companion, an irresistible Welsh Corgi named Edward. Tyler's Edward, possibly the book's most captivating character, is, however, more than a scene-stealer; it is Edward who expresses the rage and confusion that Macon so carefully represses. "Could a dog," Macon wonders, "have a nervous breakdown?" (*AT* 27) Confronted with his wife's anger at the senseless cruelty of the loss of their child, Macon objects: "I just feel we can't afford to have these thoughts" (*AT* 24). When the thoughts come unbidden in the night, he tells himself sternly: "Don't think about it" (*AT* 18–19). The more fiercely, however, the man represses his feelings, the angrier the dog; Edward is the id in canine form.

> . . . Edward when he snarled was truly ugly. His fangs seemed to lengthen. He snapped at his leash with an audible click. Then he snapped at Macon's hand. Macon felt Edward's hot breath and the oddly intimate dampness of his teeth. His hand was not so much bitten as struck—slammed into with a jolt such as you'd get from an electric fence. . . . there was some splintery, spiky feeling to the air. (*AT* 91)

Edward, beloved of readers as he may be, does not endear himself to those obliged to live with him, and more than one pronounces him "sick." The Leary siblings, for instance, goaded by his addiction to barks and bites, leaps and snarls, advocate getting rid of the dog or even doing away with him (*AT* 92, 162), thus manifesting that hostility of law to the revolutionary principle that Edward represents.

In *The Accidental Tourist's* chronicling of the struggle to fill the emptiness of the winged armchair with a constituted and integrated self, Macon is psychically beleaguered by conflicting forces very like the three "tyrants" Freud sees as laying seige to the ego: "the external world, the super-ego, and the id."[10] Even as the ego struggles to gratify the instincts of the id, it must admit the realities of the external world, and face up to the norms of behavior imposed by the "severe super-ego." Thus, the unfortunate ego is "goaded on by the id," "rebuffed by reality," and "hemmed in by the super-ego," as it struggles to achieve "some kind of harmony."[11] And the self can be composed only by resolution of the clash between the principle of law, product or at least corollary of the law-obsessed super-ego, and the principle of the id fighting for freedom.

Caught in a squeeze between the symbolically exerted pressures of law set down in language and the pressing if unarticulated claims of the real, Macon's self, like Freud's ego as Eagleton describes it, "is a pitiable, precarious entity, battered by the external world, scourged by the cruel upbraidings of the superego, plagued by the greedy, insatiable demands of the id."[12] His attempts to placate the super-ego are doomed because he cannot leave Edward behind and so goes accompanied by an inarticulate intruder into the realm of law. As the linguistically hyper-conscious Learys exist within an abstractly symbolic register, Edward the dog operates in pre-linguistic space: he has no comprehensible voice. As the super-ego in Lacan's theoretical models occupies the symbolic register of language, so the "real" "partakes of . . . the Id's disconcerting and unpredictable powers."[13] Lacan's "real," stands for "what is neither symbolic nor imaginary, and remains foreclosed from the analytic experience, which is an experience of speech."[14]

But help comes for Edward and for Macon in the person of Muriel Pritchett, whose "un-lawful" manipulations of language penetrate to the pre-linguistic space occupied by Edward and by Macon's repressed desires. In

The Accidental Tourist, Anne Tyler has constructed a comic narrative of therapy in which the dog-trainer—bony, tacky, undereducated—enacts a parody of psychoanalysis. At opposite poles from the orthodox taciturn analyst, Muriel breathlessly spills out ungrammatical accounts of her own youthful traumas, barely pausing to exert the requisite disciplinary pressures on an adoring if recalcitrant Edward:

> Edward stayed, but a yelp erupted from him every few seconds, reminding Macon of the periodic bloops from a percolator. Muriel hadn't seemed to hear. She'd started discussing her lesson plan and then for no apparent reason had veered to her autobiography. But shouldn't Edward be allowed to get up now? How long did she expect him to sit there? (*AT* 100)

Muriel's uneven progress with Edward can be measured in the series of her lessons. Macon's painful movement from numbness to affective rebirth is also influenced by Muriel's intervention, and its stages are marked by dreams. Encased in his plaster cast, having regressed into reconstituted childhood, Macon is dead to desire. Beyond mere libidinal demands, Macon has incapacitated himself also for psychic and philosophical desire—for awareness of the other. After sequential dreams of his dead son Ethan, in which he is forced to recognize the loss, Macon's dream life moves beyond Thanatos to Eros. Much to his startled (and embarassed) amazement, he dreams of Muriel:

> . . . he dreamed he was parked near Lake Roland in his grandfather's '57 Buick. He was sitting in the dark and some girl was sitting next to him. He didn't know her, but the bitter smell of her perfume seemed familiar, and the rustle of her skirt when she moved closer. He turned and looked at her. It was Muriel. He drew a breath to ask what she was doing here, but she put a finger to his lips and stopped him. She moved closer still. She took his keys from him and set them on the dashboard. Gazing steadily into his face, she unbuckled his belt and slipped a cool, knowing hand down inside his trousers. (*AT* 110–11)

Threatened perhaps by the dream-dawning of desire and the concomitant recognition of the other, Macon promptly puts a stop to the therapeutic process. After the shock of the erotic dream, Macon finds an excuse to banish the dog-trainer. Denying his accusation that she has been unduly harsh with Edward, Muriel retaliates, putting her case with telling indignation: "You want a dog that bites all your friends? Scars neighbor kids for life? Gets you into lawsuits? You want a dog that hates the whole world? Evil, nasty, *angry* dog? That kills the whole world?" (*AT* 123) In the aftermath of this rancorous parting with Muriel, Macon realizes his reluctance to resume his travels, even the crippled travels of the accidental tourist. He recognizes his attachment to the protective plaster and to his deadened and mummified self:

It was hard for him to imagine resuming his travels. Sometimes he wished he could stay in his cast forever. In fact, he wished it covered him from head to foot. People would thump faintly on his chest. They'd peer through his eyeholes. "Macon? You in there?" Maybe he was, maybe he wasn't. No one would ever know. (*AT* 125)

Shortly after his flight from Edward's therapy and his own, Macon meets his estranged wife for dinner at a restaurant that was "his grandfather's favorite . . . his great-grandfather's too, quite possibly" (*AT* 130). Still hampered by crutches and shielded by his cast, Macon experiences another of the novel's "misrecognitions." Glimpsing Sarah after the months of separation was, Macon realizes, "something like accidentally glimpsing his own reflection in a mirror" (*AT* 131). Sarah, for her part, sees Macon as "ossified" and "encased": "You're like something in a capsule. . . . a dried-up kernel of a man." She goes on to associate his life-denying impenetrability with his use of language, the texts he creates, "those silly books telling people how to take trips without a jolt. That traveling armchair isn't just your logo," she taxes him; "it's you" (*AT* 142). If, as Lacan suggests, "we arrive at a sense of an 'I' by finding that 'I' reflected back to ourselves by some object or person in the world,"[15] the reflection of himself that Sarah offers Macon is stifling and stifled. As feelingly as she reproaches his thralldom to order and to stasis, Sarah cannot counter his paralysis.

The dream of Muriel that so frightens Macon heralds a reawakening of the paralyzed erotic impulse and also of a deeper desire related to that manifested in a dream of his grandfather, law-giver and progenitor. Near the end of his life, Grandfather Leary longed to travel to a distinctly foreign country that could be located in no atlas or encyclopaedia. The island home he longed for he calls "Lassaque," a realm clearly of the psyche where not only does "knowledge" not "come from books but from living," but written language is forbidden as dangerous "black magic" (*AT* 145–46). The old man's yearning for Lassaque comes back to Macon when, on the eve of the day his cast is to be removed, he dreams of his grandfather telling him that he had lost the center of his life, urging him to find his wife and to flee the patriarchal domain: "You want to sit in this old house and rot, boy? It's time we started digging out! How long are we going to stay fixed here?" (*AT* 148) Having listened then to the representative of law speak out for emancipation, to the patriarch of the register of language deny the efficacy of the word, Macon must face the world without armour. Sitting in the doctor's office where the protective cast has been ruthlessly cut away, he considers his exposed and weakened leg: "He wondered if he'd ever return to his old, unbroken self" (*AT* 149).

But the unbroken self is bought with the sacrifice of desire, and the beginnings of desire had broken through Macon's defenses. As Lacan defines it:

> Desire is that which is manifested in the interval that demand hollows within itself, in as much as the subject, in articulating the signifying chain, brings to light the want-to-be, together with the appeal to receive the complement from the Other, if the Other, the locus of speech, is also the locus of this want, or lack.[16]

According to Suzanne Clément's commentary on Lacan, the first step to desire is the mirror; subsequently—"as soon as the image forms in the mirror," "lack intervenes between the subject and the reflection." Once the desire is thus conceived, "it is only the Other who is lacking."[17] Having experienced first the mirror and then the hollowed lack that the dream of Muriel had forced into consciousness, Macon must admit into the realm of words the recognition of and need for the other. Compelled by Edward's renewed violence to face the inadequacy of paternal law to control the id, Macon is forced to experience Muriel's absence as lack. Venturing out to New York on the first accidental tourist foray since his separation from Sarah and subsequent retreat, Macon suffers a panic attack on top of a skyscraper; at the same moment, Edward, abandoned at home, corners one of the Leary brothers in the pantry. It is at this juncture that Macon, recognizing lack, calls Muriel.

Once Muriel is reinstated as Edward's therapist, it remains for Macon to accept her as the means to his own cure. Before desire can be allowed to find its object, Macon must deal with that other lack that can never be assuaged: the loss of his son. He "had never," the narrative tells us, "actually said out loud that Ethan was dead" (*AT* 197). Goaded by Muriel's persistent overtures, he finally explains his reluctance to accept her invitations:

> "I lost my son," Macon said. "He was just . . . he went to a hamburger joint and then . . . someone came, a holdup man, and shot him. I can't go to dinner with people! I can't talk to their little boys! You have to stop asking me. . . . (*AT* 199)

Having thus relocated absence into the domain of language, Macon can accept the solace Muriel offers and so move towards intellectual and affective rebirth. Muriel, who has been nowhere but is nonetheless ready to travel, offers to go with Macon and show him "the good parts." And she, we believe, is just the one to do this and so to dispel at last the deep-seated distrust he feels for anything that strikes him as even faintly "foreign."

Soon Macon takes up tentative residence in Muriel's shabby house, located in what he sees as "the foreign country that was Singleton Street." There, in her world of kitchen tables and thrift shops, Edward and Macon find peace. What mattered, Macon soon realizes, was "the pattern of her life; . . . although he did not love her he loved the surprise of her, and also the surprise of himself when he was with her" (*AT* 212). In the new world of Singleton Street, a place he learns to find without direction, Macon comes to know himself as an "entirely different person. This person had never been suspected of narrowness, never been accused of chilliness. . . ." (*AT* 212)

Going out now from the squalid vitality of Singleton Street on the reluctant errands of the accidental tourist, Macon confronts yet another reflection, a monstrous other of his own creation. Lucas Loomis, encased in obesity as Macon had been in his cast, is a zealous devotee of the *Accidental Tourist*. He expresses deep gratitude to Macon for enabling him to travel without venturing much into the streets. "'Going with the *Accidental Tourist* . . . is like going in a capsule, a cocoon. Don't forget,'" Lucas urges his wife, "'to pack my *Accidental Tourist!*' " (*AT* 253) Having seen himself in the fun-house image of Mr. Loomis, Macon has a dream, which like the encounter that provokes it, confronts him with the reflection of a distorted self. In the aftermath of a rare falling-out with Muriel, he dreams of "traveling in a foreign country, only it seemed to be a medley of all the countries he'd ever been to and even some he hadn't." But this dreamland he knows to be deadened by his own manipulations of language. The landscapes he sees are, he realizes, deprived of life by "his own voice, neutral and monotonous," droning the prescriptions and proscriptions of the accidental tourist (*AT* 282–83).

Seemingly remade by his encounter with the otherness of Muriel and Singleton Street, Macon now undertakes a journey, unprotected by his accustomed devices of insulation. During a turbulent flight, he discovers a surprising new ability to ply a terrified octogenarian seatmate with sherry and reassurance. After this companionable journey, Macon realizes that he has come to be perceived as a "merry, tolerant person"; only later, when he passes a mirror and notices the grin on his face, does he "realize that, in fact, he might not have been lying to Mrs. Bunn after all" (*AT* 298). But the transformation realized in this final mirror scene is yet another misrecognition in that it leads Macon not to Muriel, but back to Sarah and an attempt to reconstitute the past. In returning to Sarah and fleeing Muriel (who reminds him of the free-spirited mother he has feared and resented), Macon makes one last desperate attempt to evade the other.

Reconciliation soon reveals that Sarah's otherness has been hopelessly dulled by her years as Mrs. Leary. She has come to believe that "there are worse things than boring" and to take comfort in the Leary rituals of double-checking rearview mirrors and the addition on credit card receipts (*AT* 308–10). Macon, meanwhile, has absorbed enough of Muriel's adventurous world-view to see fellow diners in a restaurant not as a dull and homogeneous crowd but rather as "an assortment of particular and unusual individuals" (*AT* 308). Sarah, Macon is forced to realize, may have been "used up": people may reach a point where they "could be of no further help to each other and maybe even do harm to each other. He began to think that who you are when you're with somebody may matter more than whether you love her" (AT 317). After this realization, Macon dreams of a courtroom where he travels down an aisle to find himself testifying and suspect in the witness stand:

> They asked him the simplest of questions. "What color were the wheels?" "Who brought the bread?" "Were the shutters closed or open?" He honestly couldn't remember. He tried but he couldn't remember. They took him to the scene of the crime, a winding road like something in a fairy tale. "Tell us all you know," they said. He didn't know a thing. . . . (AT 324)

This dream-trial revelation of guilty ignorance precedes the novel's last journey—a journey to Paris where the parties to the triangle converge and the novel ends. Addressing an international symposium in 1966, Jacques Lacan seized upon his experience of a foreign city to convey his apprehension of the unconscious: "The best image to sum up the unconscious," he told his learned audience, "is Baltimore in the early morning."[18] With fitting symmetry, it is in Lacan's Paris—a foreign city where he must occasionally respond to an alien tongue—that Macon Leary finally comes to terms with the demands of his unconscious. Laid up with a bad back and laid out by strong sedatives, he descends into the mock-death of a barely conscious daze. Drugged and disabled in a hotel room where the telephone is out of order, Macon dreams the narrative's final dream:

> . . . he was seated on an airplane next to a woman dressed all in gray, a very narrow, starched thin-lipped woman, and he tried to hold perfectly still because he sensed she disapproved of movement. It was a rule of hers; he knew that somehow. (AT 343)

In a spasm of pain, he identifies the dream's repressive figure as Miss MacIntosh, protagonist of *Miss MacIntosh, My Darling,* the formidably long and plotless novel he has habitually set up as barrier between himself and and all those other people encountered on journeys over the years. It causes him pain to confront Miss MacIntosh, a denizen of the verbal realm ruled by the super-ego; only in and through pain can he confront and oppose the domination of language and law, of "rules" and disapproval.

Sarah, arriving in Paris where Muriel already is, offers one last opportunity for the numbing avoidance of pain. Briskly dispensing analgesic tablets, she innocently makes her husband a dangerously tempting offer— to do his traveling for him. Macon, however, is struck with the urgent necessity of getting out of bed, and, whatever the painful cost, negotiating his own journeys:

> He reflected that he had not taken steps very often in his life, come to think of it. Really never. His marriage, his two jobs, his time with Muriel, his return to Sarah—all seemed to have simply befallen him. He couldn't think of a single major act he had managed of his own accord.
>
> Was it too late now to begin? (AT 351)

Confronting the necessity for pain—accepting that "anything was better than floating off on that stupor again" (*AT* 351)—Macon Leary at last abjures passivity and stasis. Deliberately abandoning *Miss MacIntosh* on the dresser of his Paris hotel room and then dropping his heavy suitcase on a convenient curb, Macon leaves behind him the cumbersome baggage and tight-lipped repressions of life lived in thrall to a tyrannical super-ego. With Muriel's therapeutic help, Macon has learned to allow repressed impulse, passion, and suffering to surface towards consciousness. The distorted selves reflected in the novel's earlier mirrors can now give way to the glimpsed image of the merry person who solaced Mrs. Bunn. Having allowed Edward and so the demands and rebellions of his own repressed id to be schooled by Muriel's "lessons" in life, Macon's self moves towards integration and psychic health.

Perceiving that life lived within an armoured self can offer no adventure, Macon relinquishes the habit of taking refuge and makes an about-turn towards otherness. At the moment of decision when he determines to make a life with Muriel, "he felt a kind of inner rush, a racing forward": "The real adventure, he thought, is the flow of time; it's as much adventure as anyone could wish" (*AT* 354). Macon's insight recalls Charlotte Emory's at the end of *Earthly Possessions:* life is itself the journey; we are all accidental tourists. "We have been traveling for years," Charlotte realizes: "traveled all our lives, we are traveling still. We couldn't stay in one place if we tried." (*EP* 200) At the joyful conclusion of Anne Tyler's *The Accidental Tourist*, the symbolic armchair is no longer a site of psychic absence; desire has intervened to fill the void. Having made visible his integrated self, Macon is ready for the journey of life. He couldn't stay in one place if he tried.

NOTES

1. *The Writer on Her Work*, ed. Janet Sternburg (New York: Norton, 1980), p. 15.
2. Terry Eagleton, *Literary Theory* (Minneapolis: University of Minnesota Press, 1983), p. 164.
3. Jacques Lacan, *Ecrits: A Selection*, trans. Alan Sheridan (New York: Norton, 1977), p. 4.
4. Jacques Lacan and the *école freudienne, Feminine Sexuality*, ed. Juliet Mitchell and Jacqueline Rose (London: Macmillan, 1982), p. 30.
5. Sigmund Freud, *New Introductory Lectures on Psycho-Analysis* (New York: Carlton House, 1933), p. 89.
6. Ibid., pp. 88–90.
7. Eagleton, p. 167.
8. Ibid.
9. *Ecrits*, p. 66.
10. Freud, p. 108.
11. Ibid., p. 109.
12. Eagleton, p. 161.

13. Suzanne Clément, *The Lives and Legends of Jacques Lacan,* trans. Arthur Goldhammer (New York: Columbia University Press, 1983), p. 169.

14. Sheridan, "Translator's Note," *Ecrits,* pp. ix–x.

15. Eagleton, p. 164.

16. *Ecrits,* p. 263.

17. Clément, p. 129.

18. "Of Structure as an Inmixing of an Otherness Prerequisite to Any Subject Whatever," in *The Structuralist Controversy,* p. b., 2nd ed., ed. Richard Macksey and Eugenio Donato (Baltimore: Johns Hopkins University Press, 1972), p. 189.

Anne Tyler: The Tears (and Joys) Are in the Things[1]

Margaret Morganroth Gullette

I. The Thickening of Life

Anne Tyler's narratives of adulthood are packed with *things*—well packed, with each item in a fictionally useful place, crammed with meaning. Over the years she has given us funny, troubled, complex versions of what it's like to be involved with things. They are mostly items of daily domestic use, or familiar artifacts: the three-story house with the children's rooms on the top floor, where a single family has lived forever; Jeremy's collages in *Celestial Navigation* (1974); Justine's Breton hat and family bureaus and her single set of sheets in *Searching for Caleb* (1976); Morgan Gower's eclectic wardrobe and Emily's leotard in *Morgan's Passing* (1980). These are ordinary things, yet they have extraordinary *presence*. Take the dollhouse furniture Charlotte Ames Emory's brother-in-law makes for her living room, in *Earthly Possessions* (1977). "Now on every tabletop there were other tables, two inches high. Also breakfronts, cupboards, and bureaus, as well as couches upholstered in velvet and dining room chairs with needlepoint seats. And each tiny surface bore its own accessories: lamps with toothpaste-cap shades, books made from snippets of magazine bindings, and single wooden beads containing arrangements of dried baby's breath." (*EP* 145)

This fantastically exact image of miniaturized duplication tells us nothing that realism would want us to know—it does not imply wealth or poverty, taste or talent. Until Charlotte decides to pack away the doll furniture, along

97

with all her rugs and her curtains and doilies ("What I was aiming for was a house with the bare, polished look of a bleached skull" [*EP* 186]), we couldn't guess that the category of significance is *amount*—wanting more or less. Charlotte thinks she wants less; she's always had a dream of less. To get away from these things, and of course the life they represent, she decides to run away. It's as she's leaving that she is kidnapped. She gets the trip she has been longing for, but under the gun.

Already we are in a peculiar world, in which material things loom so large, but the most important attribute of a set of objects is their quantity. The reason, in this most tangible of fictional worlds, is that her characters have to decide whether accumulation is a good thing for them or not. It's a momentous question, as it turns out, because early on in life whether you can become an adult seems to hinge on it, and later, how you want your adulthood to be—whether you want it to be stationary (with a family, house, and furniture), or whether you need it to be mobile and sparse. Through *Dinner at the Homesick Restaurant* (1982) and *The Accidental Tourist* (1985), these remain central issues for Tyler's characters.

Hers is a wavery, unfixed sign system—unlike [Margaret] Drabble's birds and flight, so conventional in Romantic imagery. To understand the way Tyler uses "things," we need to work away from the *Odyssey*. Its original— male—pattern of adulthood is one we keep in the back of our heads: it postulates a hero who spends the dangerous age warring and then roaming around rather promiscuously, without any baggage (so to speak) of family, impervious to losing goods—a man who finds it hard to get home but finally manages (Odysseus at about forty) to settle down with his family, in his fixed abode, with the property he has fought for and familiar objects about him. Restlessness is a sign of early days. Accumulations matter later. Odysseus's marriage bed, we recall, is immovable, literally rooted in the ground. In this schema, in midlife "things" mean responsibility, fidelity, and fixity. One implication of this story is that these values become more appropriate later on in life; another is that you need to age enough to appreciate them properly. This life-course plot continues to be enormously influential. Updike's *Rabbit Is Rich* takes it for granted. It dominates the young man who postpones marriage to go to Europe—the one who as an older man grumbles a bit in his den but relishes his armchair and TV set. Youth gets backpacks, midlife sixpacks.

Both men and women can now react against this traditional life-course plot, with its rigid conjunction of a particular life stage and particular values. But Tyler has been writing her novels as if she couldn't decide what the plot demanded. All the signs of it abound in her work, as I have said. But her plots assign the things and the trips to different parts of the life course. In her version, which stands the male pattern on its head, "things" come first, impatience with them later. This is or was a female pattern in our culture, but she has given it to men too: Morgan fits it and, to some extent, Macon Leary. She started using furniture and moving as signs of adulthood as early as her third novel, *A Slipping-Down Life* (1970). Gradually, her use of these signs became more intentional, extravagant, and (to those familiar with the tradition she's remaking) unexpected and delightful. She has expanded the simple category of "possession" until it gives the illusion of containing the whole adult condition (Samuel Beckett, with his bicycles and stubs of pencil, has contracted the category to the same end).

Readers soon notice that *how* her people relate to things is important— whether they inherit them or collect them, whether they fix them or merely own them, whether they yearn for them or reject them or simply forget them. Whether they like travel or can't bear it matters; and how they travel too—whether it's little trips from a fixed center, constant relocations, or a real departure; whether they are after somebody or escaping somebody; whether they are taking anyone with them or not when they go. One (Justine) is always in motion, a speedy driver whose husband tries to keep up in the second car; another (Charlotte) doesn't even know how to drive.

Tyler has been teaching us how to read the signs of adulthood her way, but she has been making up her mind, and changing it too, as she goes along. The value of the signs has flicked up and down. In one novel, nest building turns out to be the "right" behavior; but in another, for another kind of character, it is shedding the goods and moving on. Sometimes—the most radical departure from convention—possessing and journeying are not antithetical. After Charlotte walks away from her kidnapper and returns to her Ithaca, her husband from time to time asks her whether she wouldn't like to take a trip. No, says this female Odysseus, this American philosopher with a southern accent: "I don't see the need. . . . We have been traveling for years, traveled all our lives, we are traveling still. We couldn't stay in one place if we tried. Go to sleep, I say." (*EP* 200)

II. Menders and Mothers

"I mean, if you catalogue grudges, anything looks bad. . . . But after all, I told him, we made it, didn't we? We did grow up. Why, the three of us turned out fine, just fine!"

—*Dinner at the Homesick Restaurant*

Tyler has told us that as far as her own life course was concerned, adulthood was all that mattered—not childhood, not adolescence: "I hated childhood, and spent it sitting behind a book waiting for adulthood to arrive."[2] Perhaps she anticipated that it was going to be her true subject. Her project has been to discover what adulthood consists in, or perhaps, requires, and whether its requirements are compatible with what individuals instinctively and idiosyncratically want. This is not so different from

Updike's project, except that he started, resentfully, from the chafe adulthood brings after the triumphs of being a successful boy, and she started, sadly, from the internal difficulties people experience in becoming adults, even though they want to leap away from childhood and adolescence. Of course it's better to be older . . . , but every novel tackles a set of difficulties being older entails.

On the whole, she's shown that people do get what they want, or want what they get, without doing violence, making up their compatibility as they go along. Most turn into responsible adults. In short, although Tyler has no *theory* of progress (and has said she doesn't believe in it), she has been telling development stories all along, about the imperceptible and implausible ways people manage to grow up.

Hers is a quirky, unromantic view of young adulthood, in which the typical fictional signs of crossing the threshold—courtship, love, marriage, the intimate marital relationship—don't have much importance. Even more drastically for her than for Drabble, life becomes real when the children come. Adulthood is marked, first of all, by the things that come along with having a child. And because pregnancy can happen immediately and recurrently, life begins to thicken around her heroines while they're still young.

This pattern is plainly established in the peripeteias of *A Slipping-Down Life*. Evie Decker, one of the least attractive teenage girls ever to heave her bulk and insecurities onto the twentieth-century page, first claims our interest by cutting into her forehead, in the ladies' room of a bar, the last name of a local rock singer who strikes her fancy. She begins to seem like a human being one might know only after she marries him and they are about to have a baby, when she begins to worry about "finding the money for a tip-proof high chair with a snap-on tray and safety traps" and wonder which other baby equipment is "essential" (*SDL* 186). Evie comes out of her exhibitionistic adolescent infatuation—a stage of self-absorbed impulse—propelled by the baby.

For most of Tyler's women, the baby, not the husband, is the true sign of entry into responsible adulthood. "Gina was the whole point; even what Emily felt for Leon seemed pallid by comparison" (*MP* 90), Emily thinks to herself in *Morgan's Passing*. In *Celestial Navigation*, the first husband whom Mary leaves (taking their little girl with her) writes to her bitterly, "Oh I don't count I'm just a man" (*CN* 79). When later on Mary's additional children interrupt her conversation with their father, Jeremy, her face "took on that change that always happened when her children spoke. She bent her head, her eyes grew instantly opaque with concentration, and every muscle seemed tensed to listen" (*CN* 155). Tyler's male characters don't feel so intensely about the young. This is a picture of adulthood in which women star. Tyler, who has two children—and a husband she has great consideration for—has said straight out what she thinks are the most binding ties. "It seems to me that since I've had children, I've grown richer and deeper. They may have slowed my writing for a while, but when I did write, I had more of a self to speak from. After all, who else in the world do you *have* to love, no matter what? Who else can you absolutely not give up on?"[3] At some deep level, children signify the life course, like change and aging. They must be accepted, and yet they can be hard to accept.

Thus her terms here recognize a distinction, a possible tension, between family obligations and personal expansion ("more self"). This tension furnishes much of the conflict of her plots.

The tension arises because children trail along behind them all the paraphernalia of the grown-up world—not just high chairs but "income tax and license renewals . . . bank statements and dental appointments and erroneous bills" (*EP* 144), as the heroine says in the aptly titled *Earthly Possessions.* It's not the fault of the children (Tyler is particularly careful to locate the problem elsewhere), but it turns out that once you have one (or six or seven), earthly possessions turn out to be weighty. They can include other people as well as things: not just a father of the children, but (depending on which novel) brothers, a grandfather, mothers, in-laws, an old lady boarder, an old man from the mourner's bench, dogs. A whole extended family descends on her heroines: what in Yiddish is called the whole mishpocheh. "Are you keeping track?" asks one of her exasperated female heads-of-household, one of those who doesn't think she can bear it: "There were seven of us now, not counting those just passing through" (*EP* 112). Once you get started taking care, those who need care seem to proliferate demandingly. Her numerous three-generation novels are a sign of this situation, in which the heroine finds herself willy-nilly pressed in the middle.

Sometimes they bear the wild rumpus stoically: in for a penny, in for a pound. Other times they glumly or angrily yearn to escape into simplicity. In the 1970s, Tyler invented this new binary test for adulthood—whether you love to have this plenitude, or can only just barely bear it. Motherhood is either absurdly easy or desperately tense: either a woman slings a baby on her hip, like Mary in *Celestial Navigation,* or, like Emily in *Morgan's Passing,* she leans out the window to test the temperature before she takes the baby out for an airing. Tyler saw that motherhood was not in every case a happy instinct, a gift of the life course. For some it comes as a curse. She has a series of reluctant, hardpressed, unloved and grudging mothers, all from the previous generation: the two who are sure they've been given the wrong child at the hospital, and the angry Pearl Tull of *Dinner at the Homesick Restaurant,* who slapped her kids around when they were small and once yelled that she wished they were dead.

The mothers she has liked best are the relaxed and detached ones (often they are the daughters of the grudging, unloved ones, just to show how crookedly determinism works). She loves to make up little scenes that show their endless patience, their calm under stress: Mary, unflappable in a cold shack bursting with kids and wet diapers; Charlotte at the height of her frustration, kissing "the small nook" that is the bridge of her son's nose. Her kidnapper pleads with her at the end of the story to stay with him and his pregnant girlfriend: "Charlotte, it ain't so bad if you're *with* us, you see. You act . . . like this is the way life really does tend to turn out. You mostly wear this little smile." (*EP* 197) Jenny Tull, Pearl's daughter in *Homesick Restaurant,* talking to her stepson (whose mother had left him) about the father who left her and her brothers: "'You're overreacting,' Jenny told him. 'I can't even remember the man, if you want to know. Wouldn't know him if I saw him. And my mother managed fine. It all worked out.'" (*DHR* 202–03)

One of Tyler's favorite plots shows how the unready or impatient women turn into (or recognize themselves as) good mums.[4] Jenny Tull (Dr. Jenny Marie Tull Baines Wiley St. Ambrose) had started off in her own lonely mothering as a medical student with thirty-six-hour days, slamming her daughter's face into her Peter Rabbit plate, before she became a pediatrician (what else?) and the reassuring mother of seven just quoted. A person can *learn* to be the most responsible kind of adult. Jenny did it by going around watching people who did it better: "you could almost say she took notes. . . . She was trying to lose her intensity." (*DHR* 212) Two of the 1970s' novels, *The Clock Winder* and *Earthly Possessions,* are about the apprenticeship neces- sary before a woman is ready to accept family life. Elizabeth Abbott of *The Clock Winder* serves an actual apprenticeship to the Emerson family's posses- sions—by becoming their handyman—before she marries into the clan and becomes the caretaker of them all. (Inevitably, people who can fix things have privileged positions in Tyler's world. The world needs constant mending, and constant menders. And because it is a comic world, deep down, there are plenty of true adults: the needs get met.) Elizabeth was clumsy in her own family of origin, but at the Emersons she finds she has a magic touch for things. Fixing things prepares her to learn that she can get involved in the real world, risking real disaster. It's a triumph for her to realize, at the end of the book, that she can be a minimally competent caretaker, the kind of babytender whose constancy she admires. The electrical cords, smooth- sliding windows, dripless faucets and toilet tanks have provided the discipline she needed to enter the world where things are simply adjuncts of the busy, forward rush of midlife. Macon Leary, moving in with his unlikely new love, Muriel, and teaching her son how to fix a faucet, unites mending and tending. He learns to be a better father than he was with his own son: less anxious and fussy, readier to be delighted.

For Tyler, artistic creation too depends on appreciating things, and (after Elizabeth Abbott) on having an accumulation of them. Her artists are col- lectors, whose objects come to them in a haphazard, unintended way, over time. Their art evolves incidentally and naturally, like the prose of a writing spider. They're taking photos or gluing things together, without the self-consciousness that comes from knowing that these are job categories carrying some prestige in the post-Romantic world. Jeremy, the magpie agoraphobe of *Celestial Navigation,* is probably her best-known character and certainly her most archetypal artist (he is, as an artist, what his Mary is as a mother, a person with a developing instinct for plenitude). As his talent grows, his collages become thicker and then larger, and (of course) more full of domestic artifacts: a shred of a child's stocking cap, wrapping paper, "a bicycle bell, a square of flowered wallpaper, and a wooden button" (*CN* 211), a plastic banana, a baby's feeding spoon. When Mary leaves him because he missed their wedding day, he finds he wants to incorporate it all, the whole world of family he had formerly thought of as so much *clutter.* In his collage-box, he enshrines Mary, the tender, represented in his art (as in Tyler's) by the things she has swept into her care.

In describing his collage, Tyler justified—apotheosized—motherhood's minute, blinkered attention to the things of this world, justifying it not only because it nurtures the species, and proves one is an adult, but because it can be the subject matter of art. For a few wonderful unambivalent pages she inscribed her gratitude, as an artist, for the accumulation of things that comes with motherhood.

III. Surviving the Family

In fact, *Celestial Navigation* is an allegory of ambivalence about adulthood: if Mary represents family obligation, Jeremy represents privacy and the freedom to create. The one novel in which the two sides of self are embodied separately in a man and a woman is the only one that doesn't end with some image of family happiness: their requirements are too different. They can't be married.[5]

Tyler is double-minded, like so many people. (Unlike Drabble, though—from *The Needle's Eye* on, all Drabble's midlife heroines like a full house. They may not want to live in it all the time, but enjoying it is an article of faith with them. And unlike Bellow on the other side—all his midlife men want to slough off possessions.) In most of Tyler's characters, plenitude is *not* an instinct; instead, a genuinely austere self crouches beneath the burden of adult requirements. This self regards having things as a painful discipline, the proliferation of family as a mistake to be undone; even getting a spouse seems to be a kind of accident. Tyler, now in her mid forties, has written herself well beyond this transitional stage, but she has never lost the sense that some people get on the threshold, of how singular human beings are, and how odd it is that anyone should ever let her life be joined to a stranger's.

Taking up adult responsibility—children and things—seems initially to cause a lot of loose panic, as well as real anxiety. What Tyler expressed most strongly at the time of *The Clock Winder,* was how risky it would be to get involved in a family of predilection, and at the time of *Celestial Navigation,* how threatening living in that big overwhelming family was to the private self. Charlotte fears the furniture, because it became the symbol of being trapped. Apparently, Tyler was afraid that the bonding within a family, precisely at its strongest (when the children are young), was derived from weakness, repetition-compulsion. She had noticed obsessive, reluctant returns to scenes of past family bitterness. She expelled these fears mainly through *The Clock Winder* and *Celestial Navigation,* written in her early thirties. Contrast *The Clock Winder,* written just before *Celestial Navigation,* with *Earthly Possessions,* written soon after: the later novel, a first-person account with a much sassier narrative voice, revises the earlier in every way. Both describe the oppressiveness of family life, and, in both, objects are envisioned as heaping up. Close to the end, both Elizabeth and Charlotte are shown surrounded by people, taking in strays, making meals for untidy groups of eight and ten. Elizabeth is supposed to be in her element, while Charlotte does little but complain. But when Charlotte comes back and settles down after being kidnapped, the return seems appropriate—this is the life she has deliberately chosen. Tyler doesn't convince us that the Emerson family can be a desirable place for Elizabeth to dwell. *The Clock Winder* denied Tyler's fears at the level of structure but revealed them in its violent atmosphere and details of plot; *Celestial Navigation* admitted, compartmentalized, and exaggerated these fears in the mild, withdrawn person of Jeremy; and *Earthly Possessions* brought them in as Charlotte's obstinately held but mistaken opinions about her character.

After *The Clock Winder,* Tyler immediately created her most genuinely loving and contented mother, Mary, who innately needs all those children and takes in boarders and waifs as well. And after *Celestial Navigation,* she never again created a plot to demonstrate the impasses of adulthood. Even her slowest midlife protagonists—like Morgan and Macon—are relatively resourceful people who succeed in making different kinds of lives that they can inhabit with genuine willingness. Over time, her women became braver about assuming responsibility; Tyler stopped regarding it as "interference." Elizabeth Abbott tried her best not to intervene in people's lives, and still somebody shot himself on account of her. Justine, the slapdash fortune-teller, is the first one daring enough to give advice: "Take the change," she advises her clients over the cards. "Always change" (*SC* 29).

After *Celestial Navigation,* with both fear and apotheosis of motherhood behind her, Tyler could change her presentation of the crowded maternal world of things—ease her way away from it. She has a series of rather careless and yet harmless mothers: Justine in *Searching for Caleb,* or the rather marginal Bonny of *Morgan's Passing,* with seven grown-up offspring, who "had let the children slip through her fingers in some sort of sloppy, casual, cheerful style that was uniquely hers" (*MP* 102). (And then, at last, a few men who manage to lead nourishing lives that don't center on children: Ezra, who designs the Homesick Restaurant; Morgan, who wants to leave behind the debris of family life that Jeremy has made art out of.)

Justine, with only one well-behaved, methodical child, leads a footloose rambling life in which she gradually sheds the family furniture and travels light—the kind of life Charlotte only thought she wanted. Justine and Duncan have escaped from family riches and sweetness and constraint. She maintains her serenity in their drifter's life, inventing a mobile career (fortune-telling) that uses the close observation she developed as a silent, watchful child. The suspense of the book is based on our bourgeois/bohemian query: Will they finally get tired of having only one pair of sheets and go back to the solid formal standstill life that their Roland Park families represent? It's a feminist query too: is Justine bending her will to her husband's need, without noticing her own? Tyler's answer is to have it be Justine's idea that they join a traveling circus, where he can be a mender of things and she can read the cards and advise people to go ahead with what they want.

Because Tyler came to understand how natural it was to want to get out from under the burdens of a houseful of dependents, she could become more compassionate toward the awful Mom of the previous generation. Pearl Tull mellows as her children become independent adults: her fierce resentments fade; she worries about how the children have turned out, and blames herself. Tyler does question her own long-term optimism (Pearl is eighty-one when she's having these thoughts), and the hardest questions come up in *Dinner at the Homesick Restaurant,* particularly in the son Cody's chapter, "This Really Happened," which is told from the point of view of *his* son, Luke, exasperated by the way his father hangs on to his catalog of childhood grievances. But she comes down on the side of her early view, from *The Clock Winder,* that even minimal maternal competence is something to admire, when you consider the alternative. . . . Elizabeth Abbott has a revelation at the end of the book about what species continuity requires:

For every grownup you see, you know there must have been at least one person who had the patience to lug them around, and feed them, and walk them nights and keep them out of danger for years and years without a break. Teaching them how to fit into civilization and how to talk back and forth with other people, taking them to zoos and parades and educational events, telling them all those nursery rhymes and word-of-mouth fairy tales. Isn't that surprising? People you wouldn't trust your purse with five minutes, maybe, but still they put in years and years of time tending their children along and they don't even make a fuss about it. (*CW* 274)

Even Beck Tull, who did not put in his time, can be shown as no worse than a negligible guest when he returns belatedly, a man adequately punished by his self-made exclusion from his children's lives.

Tyler likes to show little kids getting sturdier despite their parents: Luke running away from Cody and then being so relieved that his father loves him and knows Luke is his son; Muriel's son getting more independent despite being overprotected. *Homesick Restaurant* asks the standard questions about environmental determinism again, but at novel-length, and long after, when the children are in their middle years and the evidence is in. "Was this what it came to—that you could never escape? That certain things were doomed to continue, generation after generation?" (*DHR* 209) Taking this long generational view, Tyler's judicious representation shows that Pearl's three abandoned and mistreated children grow up diversely. Only Jenny embraces life as if unscathed; Ezra never marries and never seems able to focus on a single individual other than his mother despite his generic kindness and desire for the forms of family "unity"; and Cody, although married and a parent, sounds at times bitterly neurotic: he catalogs the grudges. Yet even while doing a neurotic voice, Tyler let us hear antidecline notes, like the prideful reverberation of Cody's self-identifications. We're meant to see that all of Pearl's children have survived to shape some life that works well enough for them, and even Cody, who has lived in competition with his absent father, begins to understand how distorted his memory has been, and to find that the members of families are bound by more than the bitter need for revenge. This is a modest view of midlife recovery, more modest even than Updike's, and much more modest than Drabble's in her comparable book, *The Middle Ground*. But it too represents healing, achieved over time and by that token guaranteed. Healing is what now has to be accepted as the irreversible process.

IV. Knowing What You Want

It's a literary feat, and a psychological one too, after having written two novels about your fears of adulthood, to use several to argue that family and things (the more the better) are your highest value, and also write a book or two in which you show that people just as likable prefer to travel light.

What Tyler discovered is that neither the old male life-course pattern of wandering followed by stability, nor her new female pattern of maternal plenitude followed by restlessness, would stand up as a universal idea for the middle years. Instead, what she has been developing in this series of interargumentative texts is a discourse about true and false desire.

They are slow learners, these characters of emphatic naturalness, who talk as if they didn't know we were eavesdropping on them. They have so little self-consciousness that what they finally learn, in unastonished surprise, about their need for plenitude or simplicity, carries immense conviction. Justine goes on believing she wants to carry her uncle Caleb Peck along on her rapid voyage through life, not realizing that she has as much Peckness as she needs in her husband and her Breton hat. Jeremy thinks he wants only the claustration of artistic production, without guessing that he really needs to marry Mary's world of things. Charlotte, likewise, goes on mistakenly planning to depart, when her life in one place has been "blessed with eventfulness" (*EP* 64), the condition she has always truly admired. "Oh, I've never had the knack of knowing I was happy right while the happiness was going on" (*EP* 189), she complains retrospectively.

These protagonists in the marriage novels of 1974 to 1977 already have what they want, if they only knew it. But since then Tyler has written more about characters who decide they want something new—who leave everything and start over. Unlike Evie and Mary (who move away from their men out of anger, in reaction to their behavior), these older characters move toward new people, new self-conceptions, new roles. And Tyler makes the move seem easier. These changes in her fiction arose out of and consolidated a considerable development in her own attitude toward desire. After she showed Evie Decker cutting her forehead, Tyler shied away from describing a strong will, because she saw it as disruptive. This is an odd reluctance for a Bildungsromancier, an association that (as in Updike's case too) has to be overcome. Tyler has managed this task gradually. In *Searching for Caleb* Duncan and Justine inadvertently harm her parents by going after each other so resolutely, but they themselves don't suffer long-term harm. Recent midlife characters like Morgan and Macon struggle and hurt someone to get what they want, but the harm is ephemeral, the will benign. Perhaps it was easier for Tyler to make this change because she has attributed willfulness mainly to (older) men who don't have childcare responsibilities. And ambition, ruthlessness—attributes that Drabble has given to some of her strong-minded women—have appeared in Tyler marginally, in characters like Cody. Morgan disarranges lives momentarily in order to make people see what they really want: Emily's ex gets the kind of life that requires three-piece suits, and Morgan's gets a new man she doesn't find as tiresome as Morgan. Macon has to leave his wife too, but only after she left him, and then with a hint that some relationship between them will continue. There's no ferocity in desire, and very little evil in Tyler's private worlds (Vietnam happened, but offstage, while Jenny Tull was in medical school). It's not *getting* what you want that Tyler posits as the problem of adulthood: it's knowing what you want.

Each time it takes a whole plot for the main character to discover what is personally right, moving rather unconsciously through the long span of years. Progress brought about this way may take a long time: *Morgan's Passing* begins in 1967 with Gina's birth and ends in 1979 (when she has gone to live with her father); *Dinner at the Homesick Restaurant* starts with Pearl's recollection of 1931, and ends on the day of her funeral in the fall of

1979. Aging (fictional time passing) settles many questions. Earlier, in *Searching for Caleb* (which looks back over all of Justine's life) or even *Morgan's Passing,* length of reported time was a sort of apology to unseen adverse powers—first parents, and later the child Gina—for having been persistent enough to make things come out right in the end. It provided a way of dealing with guilt without mentioning guilt, a plausible reason for needing to write long progress narratives as well as progress narratives that cover long spans of time. The second time Tyler handles the divorce-with-a-happy-ending story, in *The Accidental Tourist,* it doesn't take as long to get the man into the arms of his new love; but then, *she* pursues *him.*

In general, starting with *Earthly Possessions* in 1977, Tyler has been unapologetically treating the midlife *bildungsroman* as a wonderful patient form. Hers don't have Jenny Tull's bravado—"We turned out . . . just fine!"—yet somehow, life as inscribed therein leaves people in a better state by the end. It's not clear *how*: some luck, some slow cure, some reinterpretation, some shrouded aims, some deserving, and then, a moment of choice. "'Isn't happiness expecting something time is going to bring you?'" Cody asks in *Homesick Restaurant* (*DHR* 256), in a long disquisition about progress and decline attitudes toward time. He, who stole his brother's girlfriend by assiduous wooing, expresses the view that happiness is merely a waiting game. In general, in this gentle world, we're asked to focus on the period of preparation for knowing and choosing. Then the moment itself is muted—only the outcome of what has gone before. Tyler's characters mostly go along intent on their daily ordinary necessary lives, too preoccupied to expect anything special and usually too ego-less to grab for it; they're edging toward their true desire. The midlife novel itself, sure of its genre, doesn't mind how long it takes them to get there.

V.

Tyler's people need to be a little eccentric in the external things (as every reader notices they are), to defamiliarize what they're about, which is so homey and familiar, and yet at the same time so serious and crucial—growing up though the psychosocial stages, answering philosophical questions in their plain concrete language and modern literalized ways: getting on an Amtrak car, lugging around their family bureaus. The solitary self that Tyler usually posits has a grand pedigree, from Pascal to Thoreau to Sesame Street's "Love of Chair," all arguing that a person's best chance of happiness could come from learning how to live in a room alone with a single piece of furniture. Tyler's innovation was to mesh this authentic urge with another equally urgent need: to learn how to live in the much-peopled, overfurnished room of adult responsibility. At bottom, Tyler presents the ideal pattern not so much as one chosen for us by our gender, or even determined by our stage in the life course, but as one each of us is bound to disclose in the course of our own peculiar journey.

NOTES

1. "The Tears (and Joys) are in the Things" is taken from *Safe at Last in the Middle Years: The Invention of the Midlife Progress Novel: Saul Bellow, Margaret Drabble, Anne Tyler, and John Updike* (Berkeley: University of California Press, 1988) © 1988 The Regents of the University of California. Anne Tyler is one of the four authors considered here whose novels write the life course in a countercultural way, describing young adulthood as the "dangerous age" and the midlife as a period of gains in which adult protagonists find themselves ultimately undaunted by their aging bodies, their inner weaknesses, their responsibility for their own and others' lives, or the worst blows dealt them by fate. In Tyler, as in the others, the "aging" process is seen as one of growth; privileged states usually reserved for the young (e.g., mutual love, the achievement of knowledge, or tolerance for oneself and others) are made to seem normal for the no-longer-young. Aging can feel like a cure. Heretofore, the norm in culture has been to treat the "middle years" as the beginning of an inevitable human decline process. In America and England, we have achieved midlife progress narrative for very nearly the first time in Western literature. Margaret Morganroth Gullette will continue her history of the construction of the middle years in a future volume, *Midlife Fictions*.

2. "Still Just Writing," in *The Writer on Her Work*, ed. Janet Sternburg (New York: Norton, 1980), p. 13.

3. Ibid., p. 9; emphasis in original.

4. "Like adulthood, parenthood is a relatively neglected topic in psychology. . . . we do not, as a rule, study the effects of parenthood on *parents* themselves. Thus, we study the routes whereby an infant may come to develop basic trust in the good intentions and continuity of the parent; but we do not study the equally crucial process whereby a new mother, a primipara, comes to trust her own capacity to keep an infant alive, after it has been turned over to her care." See David Gutmann, "Parenthood: A Key to the Comparative Study of the Lifecycle," in *Life-Span Developmental Psychology: Normative Life Crises*, ed. Nancy Datan and Leon H. Ginsberg (New York: Academic Press, 1975), p. 168; emphasis in original.

5. This essay was written before the publication of *Breathing Lessons*.

Welty, Tyler, and Traveling Salesmen: The Wandering Hero Unhorsed

CAROL S. MANNING

A s a young student at Duke University, Anne Tyler read and admired Eudora Welty's fiction. Welty became, she has said, her favorite author. In 1983, in an article surveying Tyler's fiction, Doris Betts suggested that Welty's influence on Tyler might be a worthy subject for study. Betts is interested in similarities in the two authors' narrative techniques, Tyler apparently having learned the methods of the short story from reading Welty and, like Welty, later having adapted these techniques to the novel form.[1] Other similarities between the two writers are evident as well. Betts points out that Tyler's "microcosm is the family, containing its two extremes, the stay-at-home and the runaway"—types, Betts ventures, "of the Classic and Romantic."[2] Previous scholars have discovered this same microcosm and roughly these same types in Welty's fiction, only they call the runaway there "the wanderer" and the two types "the Apollonian and the Dionysian."[3] As faithful readers of Welty and Tyler are aware, the two authors also share irony, humor, and keen observation of human nature. In sum, both Welty and Tyler exhibit characteristics which justify their reputations as serious and traditional artists.

In this article, without arguing influence, I want to illustrate the kinship between Welty and Tyler by identifying some intriguing parallels between two of their best works, Welty's *The Golden Apples,* published in 1949, and Tyler's *Dinner at the Homesick Restaurant,* published in 1982. These two

110

works encompass those similarities between the two writers summarized above. By looking in particular at their treatments of two "runaways" or "wanderers" in these works, however, I hope to illustrate that Welty and Tyler are not as traditional as we may have thought—indeed, that they share a subtle but incisive feminist spirit.

A familiar and appealing figure of the hero in narrative is that of the adventurer who wanders either alone or with male comrades in quest of some goal or in simple harmony with nature. He encounters heroic adventures along the way. The image has come down to us from Odysseus, is seen in American fiction in a character such as James Fenimore Cooper's Natty Bumpo, and has received wide circulation through western movie heroes such as Shane and the Lone Ranger. This hero is almost always unmarried and hence does not have the encumbrance of a wife or family to handicap his freedom. But even if, like Odysseus, the hero *is* married and with child, his family rarely enters his mind, and the author largely ignores the day-by-day circumstances of those left at home. Thus the family is seldom a concern of the reader. The story or novel is *about* the free-roaming hero and his adventures.

As civilization spread and the frontier diminished, the traveling salesman became for some writers a modern if ironic descendant of the romantic wanderer. Rather than a mysterious, lone, unencumbered hero on horseback, this wanderer is a semi-stranger arriving by buggy or car with pots and pans, cloth goods, a vacuum cleaner, or, in the case of William Faulkner's Ratliff in *The Hamlet,* a sewing machine. An implement of civilization in that he disperses its products, the traveling salesman nonetheless is often perceived in the towns he visits as an emblem of male mobility.

In her early short story "The Hitch-Hikers," Eudora Welty portrays a traveling salesman as a loner whose mobility is envied by others. The people in the towns he sporadically visits view him as a mysterious, glamorous figure. Welty herself, however, does not romanticize the salesman. In "The Hitch-Hikers" as well as in another of her early stories, "Death of a Traveling Salesman," she leads the salesman, and thus the reader as well, to realize that the salesman's roaming life has robbed him of something valuable: community, family, and love.

In contrast, in the long romantic tradition of the wandering hero in literature, the hero is in flight from those very things that Welty's early salesmen come to long for: community, family, and love. As Mark Twain seemed to recognize even as he borrowed from the tradition, the hero, or the story about him, is anti-woman. For the hero is not only pursuing adventure and/or glory but also escaping from what he perceives as the dullness of the domestic world centered on women. In the last glimpse we see of Huck Finn, he is anticipating "light[ing] out for the Territory" to escape the "siviliz[ing]" influence of Aunt Sally.[4] In Faulkner's Go Down,

Moses, the men gather at a hunting camp way off in the woods each year not only to hunt the legendary Big Bear but also to escape wife and home. And, of course, not long after Odysseus returns to his wife and home from his twenty-year adventure, he is pining to leave again. All these questers are in pursuit of the conventional romantic concept of masculinity. Ken Kesey's hero in *One Flew Over the Cuckoo's Nest* is the epitome of masculinity, the epitome of happy freedom from wife and home. As the narrator says admiringly of him, "No wife wanting new linoleum. No relatives pulling at him with watery old eyes. No one to *care* about, which is what makes him free . . . ."[5]

With her short stories "The Hitch-Hikers" and "Death of a Traveling Salesman," Welty separates herself from this romantic tradition by focusing on wanderers who learn that such freedom is not necessarily something to relish. In a subsequent work, *The Golden Apples,* she counters this romantic tradition more sharply. So does the younger author Anne Tyler in her novel *Dinner at the Homesick Restaurant.* Both writers undermine the male fantasy of the free-spirited hero by focusing on what the fantasy ignores. As viewed by these clear-eyed realists, the wandering hero is not single but married, and it is the home world he in effect deserts that the authors take as their focus. Exhibiting similar visions, Welty and Tyler portray the roaming hero—in the guise of a traveling salesman—as irresponsible, vain, and self-centered. They thus unmask and unhorse the romantic quester.

Though distinctly different works, *The Golden Apples* and *Dinner at the Homesick Restaurant* have striking similarities. Both traveling salesmen in these narratives are conceited, flamboyant men. Welty's King MacLain's conceit grows out of his inherited status. He is the handsome son of an old, established family in a Mississippi town that bears his family's name. As such, he is admired by the local folks and allowed some freedom from the rigid conventions which the rest must follow—or he is easily forgiven when he violates those conventions. Indeed, the townsfolk envy him his promiscuity, the promiscuity, like his travels, symbolizing for them his freedom. They fondly refer to him both as a scoundrel and as a perfect gentleman who always dresses in a white suit and hat and comes bearing gifts from his travels. According to one character, Mr. King MacLain even whistles with manners. Tyler's Beck Tull lacks the exalted status that King has inherited—in fact, Beck seems to have no family history—and therefore depends chiefly on his charm and good looks to get ahead. Like King, he is, as a young man, handsome, vain, and courtly. "Lean and rangy," he waves his black hair extravagantly; his eyes are such a brilliant blue that they seem unreal; and he woos women with gifts of chocolates and flowers, many compliments, and perfect manners ("he was respectful to a fault and never grabbed at her the way some other men might" [*DHR* 7]).

The women these handsome, flamboyant heroes court and marry are themselves similar yet are opposites of their husbands. Both cavaliers surprisingly undertake fast and fierce courtships of women the neighbors consider unlikely candidates for marriage. King woos Snowdie Hudson, who, being an albino, had seemed destined to remain a wallflower and a school teacher all her life. Beck woos Pearl Cody, who, at age 30, is already considered an old maid—and is six years older than Beck. The like-named Snowdie and Pearl are swept off their feet by the dashing King and Beck. Married, Snowdie and Pearl turn to meticulous housekeeping and homemaking. As one character says of Snowdie, "At her house it was like Sunday even in the mornings, every day, in that cleaned up way."[6] Similarly, Pearl concentrates on making each house she and her husband move into "airtight and rustproof and waterproof" (DHR 16). At first, it looks as though neither woman will have any children. But finally Snowdie has twin sons and Pearl has two sons and a daughter.

Meanwhile, their husbands are off selling their wares—King peddles tea and spices; Beck's line is farm and garden equipment. After a few years, King comes home less and less often and then seems to have disappeared for good, leaving his hat on the banks of the Big Black River to hint that he has drowned. In contrast, Beck's departure is sudden. After twenty years of coming home more or less regularly on weekends, he announces one Sunday in 1944 that he doesn't want to stay married any longer. He packs and leaves that very night.

In running away, both men are, like the conventional roaming hero, seeking adventure and glamor but also escape from the responsibilities, confinement, and expectations of home. Despite his law degree, King had become a traveling salesman in the first place so he could come and go as he pleases—could, as he says, "make considerable trips off and only [have] my glimpses of the people back here" (GA 253). He allegedly returns one afternoon a few years after disappearing but beats a hasty retreat when confronted with a vision of home responsibilities in the forms of his young, rambunctious twin sons on roller skates. Beck also returns after two or three years, but rather than announcing himself, he spies on his family from across the street, as King had spied on his through a porch window. When Beck sees his oldest son come out, pick up the evening newspaper and casually flip it in the air, he conveniently concludes that his family is getting along well enough without him, so he too hastily beats a retreat. Beck doesn't want to get close to anyone: "Oh, it's closeness that does you in," he says (DHR 300). Near the end of the novel, Beck tells his son that he had deserted his family because of the "grayness of things; half-right-and-half-wrongness of things. Everything tangled, mingled, not perfect any more. I couldn't take that," he says. "Your mother could, but not me" (DHR

301). So Beck—like King and the other wandering heroes—pursues his own whims and leaves his wife to cope with the tangled, imperfect home world.

But whereas King and Beck avoid the grayness of home, the authors of these works do not. For in contrast to the male fantasy that focuses on the adventures of the wanderer, *The Golden Apples* and *Dinner at the Homesick Restaurant* focus on the home world that the hero flees. By thus showing us the consequences of his desertion of his family, Welty and Tyler unhorse the hero. They further deflate his romantic image by revealing him to be an ordinary—not glamorous—man when he does briefly pop up in the narrative.

Throughout most of Tyler's long novel and Welty's complex, interrelated cycle of stories, the runaway husband is absent both from home and from the fictional scene, yet he is never forgotten by those he has left behind. In fact, Beck's and King's desertions of their families are *the* crucial events in the lives of their wives and children. Because of his absence and remembered charm, King becomes an enticing, legendary figure to the Morgana, Mississippi, community where his family lives. Envious of his freedom, stay-at-home Morganans view him as the romantic wanderer he considers himself. They create fantastic tales about him, and every woman hopes to be seduced by the handsome hero some day. For his wife, however, the situation is different. She misses and longs for her husband. Her pain is acute that afternoon when she thinks he has returned and left again without speaking to her. Running out on the porch and into the yard, she stares helplessly in the direction she thinks he has gone. Later, she secretly hires the Jupiter Detective Agency to try to find him. Whereas King leaves his family in a small town where he and the family are well known, Beck leaves his family in a Baltimore neighborhood, where he is virtually unknown and goes unmissed. In fact, part of Beck's problem, in contrast to King's, is that Beck fears he is a nobody. But whereas Beck's absence makes no ripple in the community, it causes his wife Pearl as much pain as King's causes Snowdie. Though she has come to see him as a slangy, incompetent, unreliable man, Pearl nonetheless dreams about him, longs for his return, and plans how nice she will act if he does: "He would come with presents for them and she'd be the one to open the door—perfumed, in her Sunday dress, maybe wearing a bit of rouge" (*DHR* 9).

Both wives also feel humiliated by their husbands' desertions. Initially, Snowdie tries to cover King's absence by telling the neighbors that her husband has to be away because of fragile health; he needs "the waters." Similarly, for years Pearl pretends to her children and the neighbors that Beck is only on an extended business trip. Fearing the gossip and charity of the neighbors, both Snowdie and Pearl in their pride keep close counsel with themselves. Pearl shuts all the neighbors out, allows herself no friends.

Snowdie continues to contribute to community life but maintains a personal distance.

Still another cost of the husbands' wanderlust is financial hardship for their families. The abandoned wives have to find some means to support their families, and this in a time when work opportunities for women are few. Snowdie takes in boarders, and Pearl gets a job as a cashier in a local grocery store. Once her children begin to leave home and their rooms become available, Pearl takes in boarders as well.

Just as Snowdie and Pearl suffer as a consequence of their husbands' wanderlust, so do their children. Snowdie's twin sons grow up knowing their father only through the talk they hear about him from the neighbors. In young adulthood, both sons experience marital problems without a father to turn to for advice. Wishing for his father's love and counsel, Ran MacLain begins the story he narrates, "The Whole World Knows," this way: "Father, I wish I could talk to you, wherever you are right now" (GA 157). Ran's twin Eugene leaves home, like his father, but becomes a bitter man when he does not find whatever he is searching for. Ran stays in his hometown and is dutiful to his mother but wonders if his roaming father and brother had made the better choice. Similarly, Pearl Tull's children, who are 14, 11, and 9 when their father runs away, are all emotionally stunted by his desertion. The middle child Ezra is the stay-at-home and nurturer in this case, while Cody and Jenny feel driven to get away. Beck's desertion affects Cody, the oldest, most noticeably and directly. He ever after wonders if he is to blame for his father's leaving. Addressing his father in one of his interior monologues, as Welty's Ran MacLain does at the beginning of his story, Cody wonders, "Was it something I said? Was it something I did? Was it something I didn't do, that made you go away?" (DHR 47) Because he senses that his brother is his mother's favorite, Cody especially desires his father's love and attention. He becomes absorbed with climbing the business ladder of success, to prove himself, unlike his father, a good provider for his family, but also in hopes of winning his father's appreciation and approval, should Beck ever return. Cody even enters his father's profession—he is a traveling salesman, of sorts. But what he sells is efficiency and ideas, and he is expert in his field. In leaving home, Cody is not, like Beck, seeking adventure and escape from home responsibilities. Indeed, in his determination to avoid repeating his father's life, he takes his wife and son with him wherever he goes, and he consistently aids his mother financially.

Cody and his siblings suffer doubly from their father's desertion, first simply from their father's absence and second from the consequences of that absence on their mother. Pearl's behavior toward her children is erratic. After a long day on her feet at the grocery store, she frequently comes home feeling tired, overworked, put upon, lonely, and frustrated by her limited ability to provide. Turning abusive, she takes her frustration and resentment out on her children, attacking them both physically and verbally.

Near the ends of their works, both Eudora Welty and Anne Tyler bring the missing husband back on the scene. Though distinctly different in detail, these endings are strikingly similar in scene, purpose, and effect. The occasion in each case is a funeral—Katie Rainey's funeral in *The Golden Apples,* at which the whole Morgana community gathers; and Pearl Tull's funeral in *Dinner,* at which Pearl's whole family gathers.[7] These endings humanize the runaway husbands and further undermine the familiar fantasy of the admirable, free-spirited adventurer.

In the case of *The Golden Apples,* King MacLain has returned in his old age to his wife Snowdie. At Katie Rainey's funeral, he is a shaking old man with lapses in memory who is led around by and supervised by his wife. During the funeral service, he tiptoes down the hall to pick at the funeral food, "all as if nobody could see him," and he makes a "hideous face" at Katie's bereaved daughter Virgie. He brags about his traveling life and expresses regret that he has "ended up at the wrong end" of his travels (*GA* 253). This childish, self-indulgent, vain man is not at all the mysterious figure the community has made him out to be in their tale-telling over the years. But despite the ample evidence Welty provides of his ordinariness and humanness, Morganans continue to see him as the glamorous figure of their dreams—just as earlier in *The Golden Apples,* in a story in which Welty comically associates King with a cartoon rabbit figure, young Mattie Will Sojourner willingly lets herself be seduced by a shabby, middle-aged King MacLain because her perception of him is colored by the romantic tales she has heard about him all her life. With subtle comedy and irony, Welty makes the reader see, in contrast, the unspectacular man beneath the myth.

In the last chapter of *Dinner at the Homesick Restaurant,* Beck Tull comes back home to attend his wife's funeral. Though he has not seen his family for 35 years, Pearl has made sure he is there at the end. Having him invited to the funeral may be her means of triumphing over him: she causes him, after 35 years of absence, to fulfill at least one of his obligations as husband and father. Or getting him to the funeral may be her revenge on him, for she anticipates that he will expose himself to his children as still the vain, weak man she knew him to be decades before.

And she is right. Now 79 years old, Beck still wears his hair in "a fan-shaped pompadour, still thick and sharply crimped," and he comes dressed nattily, in a pinstriped but "ill-fitting navy blue suit" with a "gangsterish air" (*DHR* 288). Despite his long desertion of his family, he seems to expect to be welcomed home with open arms and to be made a great to-do over—as though he had been away on some noble quest or is returning a hero of war. When his oldest son Cody recognizes him, Beck responds, Tyler tells us, "with a triumphant nod" and the words, "'Yes, . . . it's your father speaking, Cody'" (*DHR* 288). But in one of the funniest scenes in contemporary literature, Beck's children rob their father of his expected welcome as returning hero. Proving themselves the children of their mother, who had gone on for years pretending her absentee husband was only away on a prolonged business trip, they seem hardly fazed by Beck's presence now. Sweet Ezra politely treats him as just one of the family rather than as honored guest; Cody mockingly pretends that Beck has never been away; and Jenny seems about as interested in her father as she would be in any stranger off the street.

Just as Beck's children have never understood why their father left, neither has the reader known what exactly precipitated his departure. So at the end of the novel, through a conversation between Cody and Beck, Tyler makes sure both Cody and the reader realize that Beck's wandering has in no way been noble, glamorous, or even purposeful. It is in this conversation that Beck refers to not having been able to stand the imperfectability, the grayness, of family life. He indicates that, after one more example of that grayness, he had impulsively left his wife:

> "I was sitting over a beer in the kitchen that Sunday evening and all at once, not even knowing I'd do it, I said, 'Pearl, I'm leaving.'" (*DHR* 301)

His actions in the years that followed were just as unplanned, just as reflective of his wishy-washy character. He "[h]ad a few pals, a lady friend from time to time" (*DHR* 302), accepted whatever transfers the company gave him. In his infrequent notes home to his wife, he bragged about the opportunities opening up before him when there were no such opportunities (and Beck was not the man to make opportunities happen). In his old age, he, like King (and like Odysseus), fears that he has ended up on the wrong end of his travels: he sorrowfully anticipates that, now that his wife has died, his current "lady friend" will expect him to marry her at last (*DHR* 299).

In focusing on the day-to-day lives of those left at home, then, Welty and Tyler have uncovered the realism ignored by male fantasies about wandering adventurers. They expose the emotional pain and hardships faced by those left at home. But this focus on the home reveals something else as well: the strength of the wives left to cope as best they can. Neither Snowdie nor Pearl is faultless, despite their suggestive names, yet both display a competence and a valor that deserve to be sung. As conventional and as faithful as Penelope, both wives wait longingly for 30-odd years for the return of their wandering husbands, yet both survive and succeed quite well without those husbands. Indeed, when her husband does ultimately return to her in his sixties, Snowdie MacLain discovers that this fulfillment of her wish isn't such a blessing after all. "I don't know what to do with him," Miss Snowdie says, and Welty adds:

When her flyaway husband had come home a few years ago, at the age of sixty-odd, and stayed, they said she had never gotten over it—first his running away, then his coming back to her. (*GA* 246)

Had Pearl Tull been so unfortunate as to get *her* "flyaway husband" back, no doubt she would have experienced the same rude awakening. Moreover, had a clear-eyed realist—or a female Homer—told the Odysseus story, Penelope would, I suspect, have had the final line in that epic.[8] Having lived, like Snowdie and Pearl, more of her life *without* her husband than *with* him, surely she would have been more jolted by than overjoyed by his return. Penelope might say, with Snowdie and Pearl, "I don't know what to do with him."

NOTES

1. "The Fiction of Anne Tyler," *The Southern Quarterly,* 21 (4) (Summer 1983), 23–37.

2. Ibid., p. 27.

3. For discussion of these contrasting character types in Welty's fiction, see Robert Penn Warren, "Love and Separateness in Eudora Welty," in his *Selected Essays* (New York: Vintage Books, 1958), pp. 156–169; Ruth M. Vande Kieft, *Eudora Welty,* Twayne's United States Authors Series (New Haven: College and University Press, 1962), pp. 58–63; Alfred Appel, Jr., A *Season of Dreams: The Fiction of Eudora Welty* (Baton Rouge: Louisiana State University Press, 1965), pp. 86–92, 188–89; and Carol S. Manning, *With Ears Opening Like Morning Glories: Eudora Welty and the Love of Story Telling* (Westport, CT: Greenwood Press, 1985), pp. 89–117.

Welty and Tyler differ, however, in the emphasis they bring to this microcosm, Welty's perspective being more sociological, Tyler's more psychological. For although the microcosm for both writers may be the family, Welty tends to portray the family in relation to a community (as in *Delta Wedding, The Golden Apples, Losing Battles,* and *The Optimist's Daughter*), and thus to flesh time and place out fully, whereas Tyler focuses more strictly on the family itself (or the family and a stranger it adopts), her subject being the harms its members unintentionally inflict on one another (as in *The Clockwinder, Searching for Caleb, Dinner at the Homesick Restaurant, Breathing Lessons,* and to some extent *Celestial Navigation*).

4. Mark Twain, *The Adventures of Huckleberry Finn,* Norton Critical Edition, ed. Sculley Bradley, et al. (New York: Norton, 1962), p. 226.

5. Ken Kesey, *One Flew Over the Cuckoo's Nest* (New York: New American Library, 1962), p. 84.

6. Eudora Welty, *The Golden Apples,* Harvest Book edition (New York: Harcourt, Brace & World, 1949), p. 8; subsequent references noted in text as *GA*.

7. The last story of *The Golden Apples,* "The Wanderers," itself foreshadows *Dinner at the Homesick Restaurant* in many ways. *DHR* might almost be seen as both a concentrated and an expanded adaptation of this story. Both works begin with the dying of an elderly, frustrated woman, who accuses her child (or children) of not caring enough for her; create a complex picture of the family or community; show the return of a runaway husband; and make the traditional sharing of food by friends and family of the dead the occasion for comedy as well as revelations.

8. In her short story "Circe," Welty retells, from Circe's point of view, the Circe episode of the Odysseus epic. It is a clear-eyed realist's and feminist's translation of that myth.

Dinner at the Homesick Restaurant: Anne Tyler and the Faulkner Connection

MARY J. ELKINS

Anne Tyler's latest novel, *Dinner at the Homesick Restaurant,* begins with this sentence, "While Pearl Tull was dying, a funny thought occurred to her" (*DHR* 3). Pearl does not actually die until the beginning of the last chapter; she "lies dying" throughout the novel. Tyler may be intending an evocation of *As I Lay Dying,* a novel by William Faulkner, in which, as in this book, a mother's death brings together her family to participate in a ritual act: a funeral journey in one, a funeral dinner in the other. In fact, Tyler seems to be throwing out hints that she wants the reader to suspect a connection between the two; the neighbors in Faulkner's novel are also named Tull.[1] A close look suggests that the similarities are not limited to names and surface appearances. The structure of *Dinner at the Homesick Restaurant* is reminiscent of that of *As I Lay Dying.* In Faulkner's novel, each chapter is given over to one character's voice, one character's description of and reactions to the events taking place; the individual chapters contain conflicting viewpoints and philosophies, differing attitudes towards the mother, the other members of the family, and the task the family has taken on.

The alternation of first person narration which characterizes *As I Lay Dying* is not the narrative device at work in Tyler's novel, but the principle

119

is the same. In each chapter, the reader sees the events described with limited omniscience, revealing the consciousness of one character at a time. Consciousness shifts only with the beginning of each new chapter. The first and sixth chapters belong to Pearl, the second, fifth and tenth or last to her older son, Cody, the third and seventh to her daughter Jenny, the fourth and ninth to the second son, Ezra, and the eighth to Cody's son, Luke. Each of these chapters reveals a characteristic attitude toward the world unique to the consciousnness indicated. Each of these chapters also furthers the action, moving along for the most part chronologically, very much as the individual chapters of *As I Lay Dying* do.

Moreover, there exist interesting similarities of characterization in these two novels. Addie Bundren is a fierce, angry woman described by her neighbor Cora Tull as "a lonely woman, lonely with her pride" (*AILD* 21). Pearl is, by her own admission, "an angry sort of mother" (*DHR* 19) given to wild temper tantrums, physical and verbal assaults on her children, and isolated from her neighbors. Cody remembers "that she'd never shown the faintest interest in her community but dwelt in it like a visitor from a superior neighborhood, always wearing her hat when out walking, keeping her doors shut tightly when at home" (*DHR* 285). Both are women who withhold themselves from the men they marry, keeping themselves, psychologically at least, intact. Both find children the experience that violates them and makes them vulnerable. Addie says,

> And when I knew that I had Cash, I knew that living was terrible and that this was not the answer to it . . . I knew that it had been, not that my aloneness has to be violated over and over each day, but that it had never been violated until Cash came. Not even by Anse in the nights. (*AILD* 163–64)

For Pearl, Cody's childhood croup makes her change her mind about having no more children; she thinks, "If Cody died, what would she have left?" (*DHR* 4) But more children only increase the vulnerability. With Ezra "she was more endangered than ever" (*DHR* 4). These reactions to their children are not to be equated, but what is to be noted is that both women are radically changed, moved to passion and anger, by children rather than by marriage.

There are similarities in the characterizations of the children as well, particularly the sons. Ezra Tull, Pearl's second son, is an "innocent," patient and guileless; one reviewer of the novel compared him with Dostoevsky's Idiot, both in his own purity and in the effect he has on less innocent characters.[2] Actually, readers of Tyler's other novels have met Ezra Tull's spiritual relatives before, but so have readers of Faulkner. Ezra is not an idiot; he is slow and mild, quite a bit like Cash Bundren in his uncomplaining acceptance of whatever must be. Cash works outside his mother's window, building his mother's coffin. Ezra sits by his mother's deathbed, solid and dependable, just as he sat beside the deathbed of Mrs. Scarlatti, his surrogate mother. While Mrs. Scarlatti lies dying, Ezra does his carpentry work, tearing down walls and rebuilding her restaurant.

Ezra is also his mother's favorite child, as Jewel Bundren is his mother's favorite. But there are few, if any, character traits shared by Ezra and Jewel. Jewel is more like Cody Tull, wild and sharing in his mother's frustrations and anger. Cody is also somewhat like Darl Bundren, the highly sensitive troublemaker of the Bundren family. Like Darl, he is jealous of his brother and is untiring in his efforts to make his life miserable.

Finally, each of these families has a shiftless father. Anse Bundren is a man who believes that he will die if he sweats; he is criminally careless of his children's well-being, setting Cash's leg in cement and stealing his daughter's money. He uses others' misfortunes to his own advantage and insists on the respect he feels a family owes to its father. Beck Tull deserts his wife and abandons his children ("I won't be visiting the children," he says in response to Pearl's plea [DHR 10]) and then returns for her funeral, full of himself, claiming his family and telling his grandchildren as he "moved down the line beaming," "I'm your long lost grandpa" (DHR 289). Both women married men who were not their social equals. Now that he is "free," Beck Tull is thinking about remarrying just as Anse has. The echoes of Anse are everywhere; the reader waits for Beck to say, "God's will be done . . . Now I can get them teeth." (AILD 51)

He does not say this, of course, and Dinner at the Homesick Restaurant is not As I Lay Dying. Pearl is not Addie. She is much softer, much less perverse. She is given more opportunity to speak, allowed to live and change throughout the novel; Addie, we recall, is central to her novel, but she speaks (from beyond the grave?) only once and becomes, rather than a fully realized character, more of a narrative focal point. Pearl's anger is more specific, tied to her having been abandoned by her husband, left to support her children alone. She tells her son Cody that she was once "special," and asks, "Do you really suppose I was always this difficult old woman?" (DHR 141) She sees herself trapped in the consequences of her one great mistake. Although her anger affects the children and leaves them scarred, she does not have the power that Addie has nor the malice to use it. The ritual act here, the funeral dinner, is not something which she has consciously imposed on her family and not something which requires from them sacrifices on a par with those made by the Bundrens. Nor are her children duplicates of the Bundrens.

The structure, too, is different. Pearl's death, announced in the opening words and accomplished in the final chapter, surrounds and encloses the action of the novel. Addie is at the center of her novel. All the characters revolve around her; their words seem to emanate from her. The duration of the action is more compressed in As I Lay Dying; the organization is tighter, the center more narrow and defined. Although as one critic has suggested, the reader cannot be sure to whom the title of Faulkner's novel refers, who the "I" is,[3] the title of Tyler's novel clearly points out from Pearl Tull, away from death, and toward the healing family dinner.

Dinner at the Homesick Restaurant is not, then, a contemporary retelling of the Bundren story. The parallels between the two are suggestive rather than exact, and they call attention to the deeper thematic resemblances and dissimilarities of the two novels.

Both are unsentimental portraits of family and the bonds which join people, bonds which seem to have little to do with affection. Even need is an inadequate explanation, although it plays a role in the reliance of members of both families on each other. In each case, the author seems to suggest that the bonds are mysterious, beyond or beneath articulation (at least by these people, although Darl and Cody are sensitive to and comment on the relationships within their respective families). Forces stronger than individuals keep them together. Cody, thinking over the many unsuccessful attempts Ezra has made at "family dinners" at his restaurant, wonders why they all go every time, knowing it will not work out. Their going is as inevitable and irresistible as the Bundren's incredible trip to Jefferson; reasonableness is never at issue.

The Tull children all from time to time wish for a different sort of life, wish in fact to be members of some other more normal family. Cody compares himself with his friends:

> Look at his two best friends: their parents went to the movies together; their mothers talked on the telephone. *His* mother . . . He kicked a signpost. What he wouldn't give to have a mother who acted like other mothers! He longed to see her gossiping with a little gang of women in the kitchen, letting them roll her hair up in pincurls, trading beauty secrets, playing cards, losing track of time.— "Oh goodness, look at the clock! And supper not even started; my husband will kill me. Run along girls." (*DHR* 59)

This women's-magazine-mother and idyllic dream of family life repeat themselves in several versions throughout the novel. Jenny, having supper with her brother Ezra's friend, Josiah, and his mother, thinks of it as "a fairy tale existence," and the narrator tells us that "she ached, with something like nostalgia, for a contented life with his mother in her snug house, for an innocent protective marriage" (*DHR* 79). Even Pearl shares this longing for a better family life; when she hears a neighbor talking about a picnic her family is planning for which each adult member will bring a dish that is his or her specialty, Pearl feels "such a wave of longing that her knees went weak" (*DHR* 186).

All of this wishing and dreaming takes place within the context of their actual family life, filled as it is with maternal "rampages," brotherly malice and loneliness. Nevertheless, the reality is an inexplicable family bond with "mother" at the center, not the women's magazine mother but the real thing, complete with terrors and terrorizing. When Jenny, whose dreams are full of her mother as a witch who hands her over to Nazis, experiences unhappy marriages, she comes home to her mother. Although she has always felt suffocated in her old family house and although she cannot understand how Ezra can bear to live at home, on these occasions, the house seems "restful" (*DHR* 101), and she feels "safe at last" (*DHR* 102).

The inevitability of all this returning home seems clearly connected to Faulkner and the sense of fatalism so often conveyed by the events of his novels. One critic, speaking specifically of *As I Lay Dying*, says, "In the imagery of the novel . . . a sense of fatality is frequently conveyed through images of circular movement: repetitious, preordained and circumscribed."[4] If it is true that the movement of *Dinner at the Homesick Restaurant* is somewhat less "inexorable" than this, it is not too distantly related. The Tulls are not poor and uneducated as the Bundrens are; nor do they give voice to such baldly deterministic statements as Dewey Dell Bundren's "if it don't mean for me to do it the sack will not be full and I will turn up the next row but if the sack is full I cannot help it" (*AILD* 26) or even Cash's

> But I ain't so sho that ere a man has the right to say what is crazy and what ain't. It's like there was a fellow in every man that's done a past the sanity or the insanity, that watches the sane and insane doings of that man with the same horror and the same astonishment. (*AILD* 228)

But if the Tulls are not constantly saying, "God's will be done," they all, as they grow into adulthood, experience moments in which they seem doomed to repeat the past, to move in circles. The determinism here is of a somewhat different order. John Updike comments,

> Both novels [*Dinner at the Homesick Restaurant* and an earlier Tyler novel, *Searching for Caleb*] play with the topic (a mighty one, and not often approached in fiction) of heredity—the patterns of eye color and temperamental tic as they speckle the generations. But genetic comedy in *Dinner at the Homesick Restaurant* deepens into the tragedy of closeness, of familial limitations that work upon us like Greek fates and condemn us to lives of surrender and secret fury.[5]

Jenny Tull seems to be the child who has suffered most, or at least with less justice, from her mother's rampages and also, as we have seen, to have the greatest need of mothering. The narrator tells us that even when her mother is peaceful and serene, Jenny is on edge: "Jenny knew that in reality her mother was a dangerous person—hot breathed and full of rage and unpredictable" (*DHR* 70). She has felt the slaps and heard herself called "cockroach" and "hideous little sniveling guttersnipe" (*DHR* 70): she knows she is in the presence of an unstable witch. Years later, abandoned with a child by her second husband, Jenny finds herself slapping the child and screaming at her, "Guttersnipe! Ugly little rodent!" (*DHR* 209) She thinks to herself, "Was this what it came to—that you never could escape? That certain things were doomed to continue, generation after generation?" (*DHR* 209)

In the midst of this breakdown, Pearl arrives to care for her and her child (a solace never enjoyed by Pearl herself); she reads to Becky a book from Jenny's childhood, and Jenny moves to a different level of circling:

> Why she had loved that book! She'd requested it every evening she remem-
> bered now. She'd sat on that homely old sofa and listened while her mother,
> with endless patience, read it three times, four times, five . . . Now Becky said
> "Read it again," and Pearl returned to page one and Jenny listened just as
> closely as Becky did. (*DHR* 210–11)

Cody, too as an adult, continues to go over and over the same ground. As a child, he played Monopoly; he played it ruthlessly with a competitiveness neither of his siblings shared, cheating if necessary. Now he plays with his son Luke who takes on Ezra's role in the contest, giving up as soon as he perceives that "It's only a matter of time" before he loses. The effect on Cody is the same as the effect that Ezra always had on him. He tells Luke,

> "*Ezra* would do that . . . Your Uncle Ezra. It was no fun beating him at all.
> He'd never take a loan and he wouldn't mortgage the least little thing, not
> even a railroad or the waterworks. He'd just cave right in and give up." (*DHR*
> 224)

The same demons are haunting Cody. All his problems remain unresolved. He has transferred his self-destructive jealousy from his brother to his son, or more accurately from his brother alone to his brother and his son.

Even the dreams of the Tull family tend to be recurring dreams, inescapable. Jenny "dreamed what she had always dreamed" (*DHR* 70) that her mother "was raising Jenny to eat her." Cody's dream about his father and his own attempts to interest this man in a "salesman suit" come and go and always leave him asking, "Was it something I said? Was it something I did? Was it something I didn't do that made you go away?" (*DHR* 47)

None of these characters is oblivious to these hereditary patterns, but none of them passively accepts his or her fate either. However, sometimes the attempts to escape "fate" become appointments in Samarra, ironic and unpleasant surprises for the character involved. The best example of this involves Cody's obsession with his idea that his brother has always, and without visible effort, stolen his girlfriends. For once he seems to be successful in challenging that pattern, eradicating it by stealing Ezra's fiancé. If he succeeds in this endeavour, he will never again have to see the pattern repeat itself in their lives. His triumph is immediately spoiled by a conversation with a girl from his past, one he believed a conquest of Ezra's. She remembers her infatuation with Cody, but when he reminds her of a game she played with Ezra, she says, "I'd forgotten you had a brother" (*DHR* 165).

Cody is left with ashes and a partial realization of what has happened. He has not defeated the pattern at all; he has only misread it and by doing that he has played into the hands of the fates. The pattern is not that Ezra has always stolen his girlfriends but that he has always been only half conscious of his relationship with his brother. Because of imperfect understanding, he has always been a victim of his own attacks on his brother and now he is trapped in a marriage which rather than lessens his jealousy of his brother aggravates and intensifies it. Each time he wounds his brother, he becomes more thoroughly enslaved.

In a deterministic world, whether Faulkner's or Tyler's, the past dominates the present, quite often exercising a "malign influence on the present."[6] Addie Bundren's adulterous affair determines the relationships of her children, and the promise she exacts from her husband as a form of revenge sends them on this unbelievably difficult journey. The past event which broods over the novel, *Dinner at the Homesick Restaurant*, determining the events and behaviour, is Beck Tull's abandonment of his family. Every one in the family is affected by it and everyone's life constitutes a response to this act.

Jenny Tull abandons her first husband and is abandoned by her second. Her third marriage is almost a comic parody of the abandonment theme; she marries a man who has been most thoroughly abandoned. Joe, her third husband, describes his predicament:

> "Left me flat," Joe said cheerfully. "Cleared clean out of Baltimore. Parked the kids with a neighbor one day, while I was off at work. Hired an Allied van and departed with all we owned, everything but the children's clothes in neat little piles on the floor . . . First thing I had to do when I got home that night was go out and buy a fleet of beds from Sears. They must've thought I was opening a motel." (*DHR* 188)

Jenny marries him "with his flanks of children" because they are all "in urgent need of her brisk and competent attention" (*DHR* 213) and because the noise and confusion preclude conversation, particularly the "heartfelt" conversations of courtship which she has given up in psychic exhaustion.

In some ways, all three Tull children try to cancel out the father's act of abandonment. Jenny rescues this deserted soul; Ezra remains in his mother's house instead of moving to a room over his restaurant. Cody, the character most conscious of the wrong their father has done, loves his own son and the narrator tells us,

> (He would rather die than desert a child of his. He had promised himself when he was a boy: anything but that.) (*DHR* 299)

But, of course Cody participates in, is in fact the prime mover of, the abandonment of Ezra by his fiancé. The efforts of the other two to eliminate the "family curse" are also less than fully successful, as we shall see.

125

Neither Faulkner nor Tyler is concerned exclusively with the depiction of a determined or fatalistic world. Both are interested in human struggle and in the implications of such a world view for the human drama; in other words, given such a world, what are the prerequisites for survival, even success?

In both Faulkner and Tyler, survival and success are directly related to time and to the individual character's perception of and ability to handle the passage of time, and more specifically the relation of past to present. This paper does not attempt to take on the large question of Faulkner's use of time nor the equally large body of critical work done on the question. Rather the point is a truism: Faulkner's novels revolve around the questions of time. As one critic puts it, "The presentness of past events and emotions" is characteristic of most of his novels.[7] As mentioned before, the existence of a largely deterministic novelistic world requires a perception of time which stresses the irresistable power of the past.

The second significant aspect of time to be considered here is "natural" time or acquiescence to the temporal rhythms of nature. Acquiescence is the key word here. Characters such as Darl who try to interfere with the inevitable (getting the body to Jefferson) fail and usually fail spectacularly. Dewey Dell must also stop resisting her pregnancy and give herself over to nature's time. In an interesting article, Leon Seltzer and Jan Viscomi consider Anse Bundren as a good example of one character who not only does not resist the inevitable but ultimately triumphs because he is able to use it to his own advantage (his new teeth, his new wife). Seltzer and Viscomi see this as a typical quality of Faulkner's survivors:

> . . . spiritual triumph over the eternal forces of destruction requires a curiously static movement synchronous with nature's . . . Faulkner suggests his approval of those characters who accept the spatial and temporal rhythms of nature (often construed by them as manifestations of God's will) by delineating their success in coping with life's manifold difficulties.[8]

"Approval" may be too strong a word here at least in the case of Anse Bundren who lacks the quiet dignity of many of the other Faulkner characters who "endure," with whom he seems to be being grouped. Nevertheless, the point is well taken.

The two ideas together, the presence of the past in the present and survival through adaptation and not rebellion, suggest a third idea, the devaluation of chronology. Time best understood in Faulkner's terms, even in this most apparently orderly and chronological novel, is not straightforward; time is flux, a movement forward, backward, sideways and circular, with no clear cut beginnings or endings.

The presentation of time and its effects on characters is of central importance in *Dinner at the Homesick Restaurant* and is directly related to the survival decisions made by the characters.

Pearl Tull at eighty-five is clearly not the same woman she was when her children were younger. She is no longer fierce and angry, at least not so much as she was. More important, she has changed her approach to time. The reader learns that the younger Pearl was extremely orderly. The bureau drawers, as Cody remembers, were highly organized: "the clothing organized by type and color, whites grading into pastels and then to darks; comb and brush parallel; gloves paired and folded like a row of clenched fists" (*DHR* 42). This order intensifies upon her husband's departure as if her strategy for living through her ordeal is to keep everything else she has under tight control. Her management of time fits too under this heading: she has plans for her children, particularly Ezra, schedules for his life. In a telling incident, the old Pearl remembers with regret her younger response to Ezra's question while still in elementary school, "Mother . . . if it turned out that money grew on trees just for one day and never again, would you let me stay home from school and pick it?" She refuses saying that his education is more important. Ezra reminds her that it is just for one day, and she has a suggestion:

> "Pick it *after* school. Or before. Wake up extra early; set your alarm clock ahead an hour."
> "An hour!" he said. "One little hour for something that happens only once in all the world." (*DHR* 19)

Although Ezra never adopts her ideas about school and schedules, and never does accept her "plans" for him, the other two children are more influenced by her husbanding of time and her powerful sense of orderliness, at least temporarily.

Jenny begins her adulthood with the same intense orderliness that her mother had. Her college roommate is "exasperated with the finicky way she aligned her materials on her desk" (*DHR* 82). This leads her to marriage with a person whose orderliness puts her mother's to shame; they marry on a timetable; his plan is "that we might become better acquainted over the summer and marry in the fall" (*DHR* 88). This schedule is important since it will allow them to share an apartment at the university in the fall and cut down on expenses. Jenny finds that, like her brother Cody, she has married believing she was acting freely and then has found herself trapped:

> Having got what she was after, she found it was she who'd been got. Talk about calculating! He was going to run her life, arrange it perfectly by height and color. (*DHR* 104)

After leaving him, Jenny abandons order and schedules for good; the new Jenny leaves her brother Ezra in her waiting room, forgetting a lunch date with him. Her home is "warrenlike" filled with children and clutter; she trips over things and never cleans up. Her pediatric practice is hectic and disorderly too. She is totally changed. What has most effectively brought this change about is the failure of her second marriage. Left by a man she loved (reliving her mother's life), she found that her control was no defense against life, and she chose a new style. The narrator says, "she was learning how to make it through life on a slant. She was trying to lose her intensity." (*DHR* 212) She begins to take life as a joke, a hopelessly silly business. And she believes that "you make your own luck." She criticizes Cody for thinking otherwise and for cataloguing the little "harmless" memories from their childhood. (*DHR* 199)

Ezra, too, tries to offer no resistance to life, to eliminate intensity. He tells his mother when she questions his not standing up to a bully, "I'm trying to get through life as a liquid" (*DHR* 166). He tries to liquify life for others also; his restaurant is a place for him to mother people, to fill them with garlicky soups "made with love" (*DHR* 119), to advise them on what to eat to ease their various complaints. At his restaurant he does not serve fruits and vegetables out of season. He is the one who organizes the ritual family dinners and tries to feed them all with love. He would seem thoroughly in tune with natural temporal rhythms, the earth mother.

These two responses to life, Jenny's and Ezra's, are not without their drawbacks. Ezra's restaurant is a substitution for reality; it is in a sense a creation of a home for himself with all the elements of the women's-magazine-mothering we have mentioned before. There is no trace of Ezra's real mother here. Pearl never eats anything here, and Cody remembers her cooking:

> He remembered her coming home from work in the evening and tearing irritably around the kitchen. Tins toppled out of the cupboards and fell all over her—pork 'n beans, Spam, oily tuna fish, peas canned olive-drab . . . She burned things you would not imagine it possible to burn and served others half-raw, adding jarring extras of her own design, such as crushed pineapple in the mashed potatoes (Anything as long as it was a leftover, might as well be dumped in the pan with anything else). Her only seasonings were salt and pepper. Her only gravy was Campbell's cream of mushroom soup, undiluted. (*DHR* 159–60)

Like his brother and sister, Ezra is homesick for a home he never had.

The restaurant is just one of several homes that Ezra takes in place of, or to supplement, his family home. His friend Josiah's mother tells Jenny that Ezra "has been like a son to me, always in and out of the house" (*DHR* 77), and Jenny learns for the first time that Ezra eats supper there regularly. Mrs. Scarlatti, who sells Ezra a share in her restaurant for one dollar and then leaves him the rest in her will, calls Ezra "my boy here" (*DHR* 93). Ezra sits at her deathbed just as he sits at his mother's. In other words,

Ezra's approach to his home life is, like Jenny's, on a slant. He is discharged from the army for sleepwalking, something he knew he was doing, and could have probably stopped, but did not. He is doing something similar through all his life. This may be the reason that, on her deathbed, Pearl tells Ezra and Jenny that "You were always duckers and dodgers" (*DHR* 33).

Jenny has certainly chosen a life of ducking and dodging. She, by changing herself into someone who is at a distance from life, has effectively cut herself off from her past. Ezra gives her some photographs of herself as a child which she shows to her stepson. He says, "It's someone else. . . . Not you; you're always laughing and having fun." (*DHR* 203) To him the girl in the picture looks like Anne Frank. Jenny's response to this is indifference. Later, watching a showing of the film, "A Taste of Honey," Jenny remembers having loved it when she first saw it, but she cannot remember why; she cannot remember who she was then.

The price for rejection of the past and the choice of a distant life is a kind of hysteria. She is unable to be serious and unable to help, or even to recognize the need for help, when her stepson's problems are pointed out to her by a priest, a teacher, and even her mother:

> "Oh Jenny," her mother said sadly. "Do you have to see everything as a joke?"
> "It's not *my* fault if funny things happen," Jenny said.
> "It most certainly is," said her mother. (*DHR* 205)

Jenny and Ezra may have escaped from some of the pain but they have both crippled themselves in the process. There is no escape, at least not in trying to circumvent one's fate.

The Tull child who cannot escape intensity (and who is not accused of "ducking and dodging"), who is unable to get some distance or to take life on the slant, is, of course, Cody. Cody is in many ways the central consciousness of this novel (somewhat as Darl is); his observations are the most acute, and he is the one who undergoes a crucial change by the end of the novel. He is also the one most like Pearl himself, something Pearl does not recognize; she feels only his "unreasonable rages" and his withholding. (*DHR* 22) She thinks that "none of her children possessed a shred of curiosity" (*DHR* 24), but she does not know about Cody and his father's letters. Beck writes a short note to Pearl every few months, enclosing a little money. Before she ever sees these letters, Cody steams them open, reads them and re-seals them. Pearl never knows this, and neither of the other children is aware of the existence of the letters.

Pearl and Cody are the two who think about Beck, who see him as the "absent presence," an audience for any and all achievements. In Cody's dreams, Cody is a toddler, trying to impress his father. When they finally meet at the funeral, Cody's reaction is one of deflation:

Cody had a sudden intimation that tomorrow, it would be more than he could manage to drag himself off to work. His success had finally filled its purpose. Was this all he had been striving for—the one brief moment of respect flitting across his father's face? (*DHR* 291)

The sense of abandonment, of having been wronged, is most acute in Pearl and Cody. He shares with his mother, too, her sense of time. Like her he is always "running on schedule" (*DHR* 90): he has, in fact, taken it beyond the standard set for him by his mother. He is on schedule with a vengeance; he has become a very successful efficiency expert, and he tells his son,

> Time is my obsession: not to waste it, not to lose it. It's like . . . I don't know, an object, to me; something you can almost take hold of. If I could just collect enough of it in one clump, I always think. If I could pass it back and forth and sideways, you know? If only Einstein were right and time were a kind of river you could choose to step into at any place along the shore. (*DHR* 223)

All of the emphasis in this passage is on control: holding on to time, collecting it, passing it back and forth. Although Cody does not actually say what would happen "if I could just" or "if only," the implication seems to be that if one could manage time, one could step into anywhere necessary and fix whatever had gone wrong. The repetition of "ifs" in this passage suggests the hopelessness of the attempt and the frustrations implicit in the life of such an efficiency expert. His attitude is the exact opposite of his brother's; rather than blending in with whatever is in season, Cody is constantly trying to change the season. He tells Luke, "If they had a time machine, I'd go on it. . . . It wouldn't matter to me where. Past or future: just out of my time. Just someplace else." (*DHR* 223)

But, in fact, it does matter where. Most of the time, his unhappiness is much more clearly focused than this as he suggests later in this passage:

> "Everything," his father said, "comes down to time in the end—to the passing of time, to changing. Ever thought of that? Anything that makes you happy or sad, isn't it all based on minutes going by? Isn't happiness expecting something time is going to bring you? Isn't sadness wishing time back again? Even *big* things—even mourning a death: aren't you really just wishing to have the time back when that person was alive? Or photos—ever notice old photographs? How wistful they make you feel? Longago people smiling, a child who would be an old lady now, a cat that died, a flowering plant that's long since withered away and the pot itself broken or misplaced. . . . Isn't it just that time for once is stopped that makes you wistful? If only you could change this or that, undo what you have done, if only you could roll the minutes the other way for once." (*DHR* 256)

Here again are the "if only's"; here, Cody associates happiness with anticipation, with looking forward, and unhappiness with the past. When Cody says, "Time is my obsession," he means the past is his obsession. He never looks forward; he relives and replays the past telling the same stories over and over again to his son, recalling the same unhappy memories for his sister and brother. Even his marriage is a step backward, an attempt to "roll the minutes the other way for once."

The structure of the novel reveals this concern. Some details are repeated in various sections of the book, in the minds and memories of different speakers and in different contexts. One of the most important of these is the archery incident. The facts of the case, Pearl's having been the accidental victim of an arrow shot by Cody while roughhousing with Ezra, are reported four different times in the novel. In the three other versions,

> While Cody's father nailed the target to the tree trunk, Cody rested the bow. He drew the string back, laid his cheek against it, and narrowed his eyes at the target. (*DHR* 35)

The straightforward sentence structure gives intensity and adds to the general foregrounding of the incident. In the first sentence, as through the entire account, Cody dominates. His father appears in the subordinate clause and is referred to as "Cody's father." The gist of the story is Cody's father's foolish irresponsibility, his mother's favouring of Ezra, and his own victimage. Pearl is wounded and Cody says to Ezra, "See what you've gone and done? . . . Gone and done it to me again . . . ." (*DHR* 39) For Cody this incident is important because it is a perfect example of his having been victimized by his brother. Appropriately, it has no context here. There is no mention of the penicillin reaction, and it is not until the end of the novel that Cody, and the reader, learn that this incident precipitated the father's departure. Cody is unable to see it any other way.

Later in the novel, he tells his son another story of his mother's favoring of Ezra at his expense, and when Luke tries to suggest a different interpretation of the "facts," Cody willfully misunderstands his point and responds, "Oh I don't know why I bother talking to you. You're an only child, that's your trouble. You haven't the faintest idea what I'm trying to get across." (*DHR* 220) All of Cody's memories are suspect, for this reason, and as the novel moves toward its final conclusion, more and more characters suggest to him the narrowness of his vision. At one point Luke wakes up his mother to get her to contradict one of Cody's memories, and at the funeral, Ezra interrupts a harangue to say "It wasn't like that" (*DHR* 295).

What happens to Cody and his approach to the past has its parallels in his mother's life and death. Aging and dying have brought about changes in her attitude. Remembering the incident of the money growing on trees, she thinks, "If money decided to grow on trees one day, let him pick all he liked! she should have said. What difference would it have made?" (*DHR* 19) On her deathbed, Pearl moves back and forth in time between the present and memory; she seems equally at home in either, and the structure of the novel reveals this flux. Time shifts continually, the past and present sliding into each other with Pearl "skidding through time" (DHR 32) and constantly "mislaying her place in time" (DHR 34) and not minding. She is able to see the connections. Her attitude toward the past now is not one of regret; she does not wish to go back and fix things, but simply to take it all in. She says, "It was such a relief to drift, finally. Why had she spent so long learning how?" (DHR 34) Her attitude toward movement through time has had to be learned. She does not try to manage it as she once did; neither does she duck and dodge as Ezra and Jenny do.

The only other chapter set in Pearl's consciousness is the sixth chapter, "Beaches on the Moon," located at the center of the novel, immediately following Cody's disastrous courtship. In this chapter, the movement is similar to that of the first chapter (and dissimilar to all the others in which the movement is relatively straightforward). The sixth chapter begins with a flashback to Pearl and Ezra on a cleaning expedition to Cody's farm, not a one time occurrence. The opening sentence is suggestive:

> Twice or maybe three times a year, she goes out to the farm to make sure things are in order. She has her son Ezra drive her there, and she takes along a broom, a dustpan, rags, a grocery bag for trash and a bucket, and a box of cleanser. (DHR 167)

Several factors are at work here which give a sense of timelessness. The non-specific reference "twice or maybe three times a year," and the use of the present tense work together to lift this incident out of the everyday past and give it a repetitive, almost ritualistic quality. She does this time after time, year after year, in the same way and with the same materials. She is moving beyond chronological time. The conclusion of the chapter reinforces this impression:

> Next season she will come again, and the season after, and the season after that, and Ezra will go on bringing her—the two of them bumping down the driveway, loyal and responsible, together forever. (DHR 186)

Between the beginning and end of this chapter, contained within this timelessness, are her memories of Cody's marriage, almost all of them unhappy, none of them overwhelming or obsessive.

Pearl spends her last days with Ezra, listening to him as he describes to her the photographs and diaries from her youth. The photographs are very important in this novel; they are, of course, the perfect image of the presentness of the past. As Cody recognized, they stop time for a moment; the past exists in those photographs just as the photographs exist in the present. What Cody has not recognized is that the past and present are equally alive in them (the girl with the Anne Frank face is Jenny, duck and dodge though she may); the key is to find the connection. It is to find the connection that Pearl goes over and over them, and for that she does not need her eyesight.

She sees in them and hears in the words from the diaries what Ezra who reads them cannot hear. Ezra sees that her life as a girl was full of possibility but he can only conclude that "nothing has come of it" (*DHR* 268). The knowledge makes him too tired to read further. Pearl, however, knows better. Later, Ezra reads her the following entry:

> The Bedloe girls' piano scales were floating out her window . . . and a bottle fly was buzzing in the grass, and I saw that I was kneeling on such a beautiful green little planet. I don't care what else might come about, I have had this moment. It belongs to me. (*DHR* 227)

Pearl requires no further reading. She understands what Ezra does not, that life is a reverberating moment and not a plot unfolding and leading to a happy or unhappy ending.

It is to Tyler's great credit that the novel is hers and not merely a pale imitation or reworking of Faulkner's novel. The homage to Faulkner is there, of course; Tyler locates her novel in a tradition of fiction which probes the psychological dynamics of a family, goes beneath the surface pieties to the underlying mysteries. Like Faulkner, she sees and shows the damages done as well as the loyalties created, the ways in which family members use their privileged positions and intimate knowledge of each other to their own benefit.

Like Faulkner, she understands the complications and the human impulse to gloss them over. Cody, listening to the minister at his mother's funeral offering the obligatory cliches and consolations ("a devoted wife and a loving mother and a pillar of the community" [*DHR* 285]), suggests to himself a different version of her "long full life":

> . . . [that] she'd been a frantic, angry, sometimes terrifying mother and that she'd never shown the faintest interest in her community but dwelt in it like a visitor from a superior neighborhood, always wearing her hat when out walking, keeping her doors shut tightly when at home (*DHR* 285).

Tyler dramatizes the inadequacies of both of these perceptions of "family life"—Cody's as well as the minister's. Throughout the novel, the family structure shifts, regroups, and emerges altered but intact. At the end of the novel Cody's unkind revelations to his father have driven the old man from the funeral dinner. Cody is shamed into joining the others in trying to find him. He sees a man who he thinks is his son, but who in fact is his father. This is an odd mistake to make since Luke is said to resemble Ezra and Beck and Cody share a resemblance; the four male characters blend for a moment into one, long enough to allow the father his moment, his version of the desertion. At the end of the explanation he says:

> I do believe that all these years, anytime I had any success, I've kind of, like, held it up in my imagination for your mother to admire. Just take a look at *this*, Pearl, I'd be thinking. Oh, what will I do now she's gone? (*DHR* 302)

The connection here is striking. For Beck, Pearl was the "absent presence" as he was for her and Cody; this allows Cody to see things at least for a moment from another perspective than his own and to see his mother clothed in something other than witch's garb. The novel ends with Cody's revised memory of the archery incident:

> He remembered the archery trip and it seemed to him now that he even remembered that arrow sailing in its graceful, fluttering path. He remembered his mother's upright form along the grasses, her hair lit gold, her small hands smoothing her bouquet while the arrow journeyed on. And high above he seemed to recall, there had been a little brown airplane, almost motionless, droning through the sunshine like a bumblebee. (*DHR* 303)

Not only has the vista widened here; Cody finally looks up to the sky and lets in some light. Here, Cody's mother is the young girl of her own memories. The language of this impressionistic idyllic description recalls Pearl's moment in time with the green grass, the floating music, and the buzzing of the bottle fly. Cody has finally managed to step into the river of time at some other moment; past becomes present. Obsession gives way to perspective.

The ending is not Faulknerian: the determinism is downplayed, the optimism is limited but unmistakeable. The family may even enjoy, at last, a dinner together (although Beck is threatening to leave before the dessert wine). The Tull family members are not so isolated from each other as the Bundrens. They understand a bit more fully that making it through life— even as a liquid—is something of a joint venture in substance as well as in form. The ghost of Anse Bundren may be sitting at this table waiting for a chance to try out his new teeth, but he has no use for them here at the Homesick Restaurant, where the specialities of the house, made with love and a secret ingredient ("that you'd only share with blood kin" [*DHR* 293]), are soups: steamy, garlicky, improbable but nourishing, homemade soups.

NOTES

1. William Faulkner, *As I Lay Dying* (1930) (New York: Random House New Edition, 1964); subsequent references noted in text as *AILD*.

2. Benjamin DeMott, "Funny, Wise and True" [rev. of *Dinner at the Homesick Restaurant*], *The New York Times Book Review*, 14 March 1982, p. 14.

3. Stephen M. Ross, "'Voice' in Narrative Texts: the Example of *As I Lay Dying*," PMLA, 94 (March 1979), 308.

4. Charles Palliser, "Fate and Madness: The Determinist Vision of Darl Bundren," *American Literature*, 49 (1977/78), 625.

5. John Updike, "On Such a Beautiful Green Little Planet" [rev. of *Oh, What a Paradise It Seems* by John Cheever and *Dinner at the Homesick Restaurant*], *The New Yorker*, 58 (5 April 1982), 194.

6. Palliser, p. 632.

7. James H. Matlack, "The Voices of Time: Narrative Structures in *Absalom, Absalom,*" *Southern Review,* 15 (Spring 1979), 341.

8. Leon F. Seltzer and Jan Viscomi, "Natural Rhythms and Rebellion: Anse's Role in *As I Lay Dying,*" *Modern Fiction Studies,* 24 (Winter 1978–79), 557.

Private Lives and Public Issues: Anne Tyler's Prize-winning Novels

Susan Gilbert

Anne Tyler, behind the now significant bulk of eleven novels, the last two winners of America's most prestigious prizes for fiction, the National Book Critics Circle Award for *The Accidental Tourist* and the Pulitzer Prize for *Breathing Lessons,* commands a different position and a far broader audience than she had even a few years before these two works and the movie version of one of them achieved such popularity. These novels are recognizably from the same hand that shaped her first nine novels, and have been praised for qualities long recognized in her work: for her "warmth" and "effortless" prose;[1] for her "depth" and "compassion";[2] for the sense of affirmation in her work, "the resilient spirit that rescues us from moments of despair";[3] for the fact that "Miss Tyler isn't afraid to be sentimental . . . and she isn't afraid to be hopeful";[4] for the "utter absence from her work of a fashionable contempt for life."[5] Though Tyler's familiar plot lines of journeys and returns and her large subject of familial relations remain prominent in her two most recent novels, both *The Accidental Tourist* and *Breathing Lessons* are lighter in tone and significantly more topical than her earlier novels.

Tyler has repeatedly asserted that she is a private person who writes of private lives. Most critics assent and treat her writings in this vein. The judgment recurs in reviews of the latest two. She is labelled a "domestic novelist"[6] and a writer of psychological novels "in which events have what

Eudora Welty once called 'a private address.' "[7] Tyler's novels, some have observed, are a-historical, her characters so self-absorbed that they seldom see the connections or implications of their lives with or for others.[8] Often, discussions of her work imply that certain lives are private, that public affairs affect only parts of the population. Social scientists argue that all human beings and many non-human beings are affected, to whatever degree they are conscious of it, by the movements of the tribe. Tyler has observed of her work that she is "populating a town;"[9] one may question the paradox of a "town" of all "private" persons.

That Tyler's characters persist in ignorance of or indifference to social debates around them is not the same thing at all as imagining that their creator never reads the papers or watches the evening news. Nor does one imagine that the social level of Tyler's heroines who are working class or poorly educated has any resemblance to the educated professional class of Ms. Tyler. But her last two prize-winning novels bring her subjects closer to immediate issues of American political debate than her work has been before without the characters or, if the reviews are apt, her readers seeming to notice.

One could wonder in what spirit Tyler sharpened her focus, whether she intended readers to respond or imagined that none would notice how topical her books have become.

For more than two decades, reviews of Tyler's work touched but gingerly on the political implications of her pervasive subject, "the family," though for her lifetime issues about family and definitions of what families are or ought to be have carried enormous weight in debate on every political issue: tax policy and tax rates and exemptions, medical care for young and old, welfare reform, drug policies and wars. And they form the core of most issues addressed by rightist religious groups.

The Accidental Tourist and *Breathing Lessons,* though still in the main domestic novels, direct three glancing blows and one very palpable hit at the most volatile political issues of the eighties: gun control, crime in the streets, the failures of American public education, and abortion. To her characters these never cease to be private issues, sources for private and passive grief, not causes for action or organization or moral choice. Almost all Tyler's characters agree, more by ignoring the question than by assent, that politics are pointless. They don't go so far as to reject political action, whether from despair or any other motive. They seem unconscious of it. But should one assign to her characters' choices a political response, they would probably turn out consistent with conservative or reactionary attitudes.

Tyler's work, from the first, has utilized a contrast of neighborhoods. Heroes and heroines marry or mate, pair up somehow across social and economic lines. In *The Accidental Tourist,* Macon Leary from Roland Park, an old, wealthy suburb, takes up with Muriel, from a street of row houses in south Baltimore. This pattern was in her earliest novel, *If Morning Ever Comes,* where the physician husband-father, with a large house and large family on the "right" side of town, had a mistress and illegitimate child on the "wrong" side of the tracks. The pattern was there before Tyler came to Baltimore and made its neighborhoods the focus of her works, the town she is populating. *Searching for Caleb* is built around the contrast of Pecks from Roland Park who stay at home and those who take to looser, rougher environs; the young runway Pecks, children of Roland Park's affluent atrophy, live almost as gypsies among circus people. The hero of *Morgan's Passing* similarly flees the respectability of his large house and large family to discover adventure and new life in the streets of Baltimore.

Circulated at the conference on Tyler's work held in Baltimore in April, 1989, the *Baltimore Towne Magazine* contained an illustrated essay by Mary Anne Brush on "The Two Worlds of Anne Tyler," with pictures and descriptive passages from her books about the neighborhoods of Roland Park and inner city row houses.[10] Roland Park is green, its big houses widely spaced and its people distant from each other. It is wealthy and stable to the point of stagnation or decay. The city of row houses, if it also decays, does so with less peace. And though it is also often "stagnant" (*CN* 6), it may possess the opportunity for newness which Roland Park resists. Macon's grandfather in *The Accidental Tourist* asks him, "You want to sit in this old house and rot, boy? It's time we started digging out! How long are we going to stay fixed here?" (*AT* 148) When he becomes friends with Muriel, Macon decides that what matters to him is the "pattern of her life" and "the surprise of her, and also the surprise of himself . . . with her. In the foreign country that was Singleton Street, he was an entirely different person. This person had never been suspected of narrowness, never been accused of chilliness . . . ." (*AT* 212)

The pictures in "The Two Worlds of Anne Tyler" pick up her phrases. Roland Park holds "deep curly shadows and . . . pools of sunlight," houses "dark and cool and dappled with sunshine," streets "steadily greener and cooler," and an atmosphere "all rustling with trees and twittering with birds." It is safely removed from the other Baltimore with its "ashy smell of . . . factories"; its "labyrinth of littered, cracked, dark streets"; its "murky alleys and stairwells full of rubbish and doorways lined with tattered shreds of posters"; its neighborhoods "running down"; and its dwellings "split into apartments and gone over to colored and beatniks, and . . . even boarded up, with city notices plastered across the doors."[11]

Two worlds, one of trees, birds, lawns, wealth, private schools, and comfortable, if stagnant, lives; the other one of litter, darkness, clutter, fear, deserted boarded-up houses, doorways lined with tattered shreds of posters, high school drop-outs, teen-age pregnancies, fatherless children.

In the movement in Tyler's fiction, the happiest changes involve moves from the stagnant world of wealth to the other side of town, exchanging respectability for spontaneity and love outside the law's confines. This has been viewed for the most part as without political dimension. "Stagnant" is not read as "reactionary"; "fluid" never means "liberal."

Mary Anne Brush, after pointing out the obvious contrasts of the neighborhoods' material conditions, states that Tyler's thesis is that "life" in its essentials is the same everywhere: that Tyler "creates a sense of equality between the two"; that in both places "she reveals the pathos and futility of her characters' lives"; that "[t]his is the human condition, according to Anne Tyler, and it is this vision that unites the two worlds of her fiction."[12]

No one argues that Tyler's vision of life is full of its pathos; but about its futility—or possibility for joy—critics do argue. Clearly, she brings the worlds together in private resolution, in the kitchens or bedrooms of her characters' insular lives. What has not been much noted, though, is that this vision serves a static, politically conservative line on life, a nostalgic vision of an America of private houses and lawns, kept or unkempt, despite the fact that Tyler's use of headline news has become more insistent. Critics rightly refrain from complaining about what is absent from her work; newsworthy crises are not missing but are increasingly important in her last two novels. However unaware the characters remain of political currents in their town, the author has woven into their stories issues prominent and divisive in neighborhoods like Roland Park and inner city Baltimore.

In *The Accidental Tourist* Macon, leaving the tree-lined streets of Roland Park to enter "the labyrinth of cracked, dark streets in the south of the city," wonders "how Muriel could feel safe living here" (*AT* 198). The popular film version of this book features a scene in which he watches Muriel's son Alexander walk up an alley, a frail, slight child, the likely prey of bullies in a lawless place. Movie and book are imbued with the sense of peril.

Ideological criticism is at a perilous point here, too. Danger is not confined to the streets and alleys of south Baltimore. Streets and fear of streets figured largely in Tyler's fiction a decade before it became a deliberate ploy in a presidential campaign to play upon such fear. Macon fears the "clusters of people [who] lurked in the shadows—young men drinking out of brown paper bags" (*AT* 198). Readers of the book and viewers of the film saw over and over that same year the face of one of "them" flashed on television screens to provoke their fears. If Tyler's use of streets to evoke fear is older, deeper, and broader in concept than the 1988 presidential race, does it nonetheless remain separate from its timely context?

In this novel a fear of the street was the agent of Macon's initial despair. Long before the actual dreadful event which took his son and far from the human danger of south Baltimore's streets, he watched Ethan run into the street and had a vision of his being instantly killed.

To other Tyler characters, streets have represented a still larger, less well-defined fear. They figure prominently as intermediary vehicles which some enter with zest for whatever awaits them and which others, terrified, dare not enter. Her treatments of several characters' fears of the streets of Baltimore afford interesting examples of the varied ways irrational and rational fear controls human behavior.

The artist hero of *Celestial Navigation,* Jeremy Pauling, fears entering the streets and seldom leaves home. Like Tyler, he seeks to make great art of clutter, left-over bits and pieces of this and that. He fears life in the raw and dares not face its unexpected. He seems to fear life because away from its million daily shocks his sensitive nerve receptors have not become callous or inured. He remains in awe of life and is able in his art to convey this awe.

Macon Leary's fears are more concrete. On any street a child is vulnerable to sudden death; in the dark shadowy streets of south Baltimore all sorts of dangers may lurk. Eventually, Macon overcomes his fear: "Singleton Street still unnerved him with its poverty and ugliness, but it no longer seemed so dangerous. He saw that the hoodlums . . . were pathetically young and shabby . . . , an uncertain, unformed look around their eyes. He saw that once the men had gone off to work, the women emerged full of good intentions and swept their front walks" and called out to children skipping school (*AT* 234). To what degree such realization impresses readers or viewers of the film and reduces their fear of dark streets and their inhabitants is not easy to assess.

Read together, Pauling's and Leary's fears may present opposing comments on the psychological causes underlying the factor of fear of the streets in party politics. Read in one direction, these may suggest that all such fear of the other is pathological fear of life's diversity and promise and is rooted in insecurity, in diseased, not rational minds. Read the other way along the spectrum, one may be seeing the irrationality of Pauling's self-absorbed fear enter the safe respectability of common sense choices, the everyday ground of behavior where actions reinforce barely articulated premises, the ordinariness of behavior in which suburbanites lock their car doors as they drive through south Baltimore, or south Chicago, or the south Bronx.

Which way, right to left, or left to right, do we suppose the many readers and viewers of *The Accidental Tourist* interpreted Macon's fear of streets? Did they notice that the story ends on a street, this time a strange street leading somewhere new, even if it's glimpsed but dimly through a rain-speckled windshield? Macon, like Morgan leaving behind Roland Park, has entered streets aglow with brilliant possibility.

Two other judgments of Roland Park suburbanites figure briefly in the work. One of Macon's brothers refers to Muriel as "this Muriel person," observing from his social vantage point the woman who has no place among the families and social strata of Roland Park, and Macon rebukes him for it.

Discovering that Alexander cannot subtract in the second grade, Macon proposes to send him to private school—the usual suburban response to declining public city schools—and no one rebukes him for it. His offer occasions a scene between him and Muriel; her concern is that he may walk out on her and abandon Alexander, not that his private solution is socially irresponsible. Who among the readers of this book found this jarring or the hero less sympathetic?

The Accidental Tourist, if it ends in choice, in Macon's decision to be with Muriel and Alexander, began in accident, the senseless death of his son, "murdered in a Burger Bonanza": "It was one of those deaths that make no sense—the kind where the holdup man has collected his money and is free to go but decides, instead, first to shoot each and every person through the back of the skull" (*AT* 18). It ran through Macon's mind to "blame" someone: the camp, the campmates, his wife for sending him to camp, himself for agreeing, the boy for going; but he concludes, "Don't think about it" (*AT* 19).

Before such sorrow even heartless ideological criticism should falter. But the body of Tyler's work emphasizes the accidental nature of life, assigns wit and wisdom to private modes for coping, and diminishes to irrelevance the application of human intelligence and energy to organizing society to provide for the common safety or promote the general welfare, to make the streets safer, to limit the proliferation of guns, to improve city schools so second graders can learn to subtract.

Even as I write, the governors of fifty states are assembled in summit to determine whether American efforts at mass public education can be revived and not abandoned, and columnists and cartoonists depict the president wringing his hands at the public's and the media's refusal to see plainly that the thousands who die yearly from guns die accidental deaths, die from acts of God, die from causes unamenable to legislation or leadership. Where does the attitude of the hero of this popular movie and prize-winning book fit into the debate about how many deaths like Ethan's are someone's "blame" or responsibility, the result of human action or inaction, collective as well as private?

Tyler seems intrigued by the possibilities of turning her ideas inside out, and she achieves subtlety through alternation and juxtaposition. Like her plots—where in one book characters run away and then come home, in the next come home and then run away—the works present interesting alternations of passive and meddlesome heroes to whom she alternately ascribes endearing and terrifying qualities.

Unlike the termagant Pearl Tull of *Dinner at the Homesick Restaurant,* the heroine of *Breathing Lessons* is meddlesome in ways mostly tiresome and ineffectual. But in a central scene she intervenes to rescue her son's teen-aged girl friend from an abortion clinic. She promises her that the boy loves her, will indeed be a loving father to the child, and is at work on a cradle for the baby. The cradle does it. And the child becomes the focus of Maggie's emotional longing and her scheming throughout the day of the novel, which has some of the flavor of a soap opera, a sort of "Days of Our Lives."

Tyler draws children attractively. Hardly a reader could wish the little girl, Leroy, into non-being. And the protestors outside the abortion clinic, a swarming, angry mob of "Right to Lifers," like all group people in Tyler's world, are drawn in savage caricature.

Does it or does it not matter "really" to readers of America's Pulitzer Prize winning novel in the year of the possible overturning of Roe v. Wade that the story and emotional weight of the book vindicate foes of abortion, that the book's "acceptance" is most basically an "acceptance" of life? Does a writer who centers her work in the most divisive political issue of her day remain a private person telling stories of private lives?

Beneath the polish of her prose, the sparkle of her humor, these two novels present a vision that no one is responsible for the safety of the streets of Baltimore, no one is responsible for the quality of education in the schools there, no one could responsibly choose a better life for a young woman than that of a pregnant teenager, a high-school drop-out dreaming of a faithful husband and a cradle for her baby. Only meddlesome, silly people try to change things. The wise see to the unchanging heart of things and accept. Beyond change are the streets, the schools, the drop-outs, the disappearing husbands, the children without fathers, the teenage mothers unable to provide for themselves or for the children they bear.

Were these concerns anywhere in the consciousness of the critics who extolled these books? They are far from her best work. *Dinner at the Homesick Restaurant* brought deserved acclaim and understandable calls for more recognition for Tyler's work. That prizes often lag behind the worth of a body of work is a truism; that they often reflect a political climate is another.

To what, in a readership engaged in debate over guns, crime, safety, schools, abortion, do these books appeal as they pick up issues only to dissolve them as causes for concerted action? to the sense of loner in each? to an isolationist mentality accompanying the materialism of a "me generation"? No one finds Tyler's characters to care a fig about money. But few of them care about much outside the range of what they see or touch in a moment as they live within houses where currents of history pass them by.

Ira in *Breathing Lessons* has the sense that life has passed him by. He resents his wife's failure to feel this. Not articulated is that what is missed and might have been of value to him would have been consciousness of his place in a town. When Tyler's characters experience epiphanies, moments when they see through to the beauty of their lives, they are in fields or a meadow, or weeding a garden. These are the loci of the moments of epiphany in *Dinner at the Homesick Restaurant* for Pearl and her son Cody. Equally cut off from a town is the scene of Macon Leary's epiphany in *The Accidental Tourist* in a restaurant high above the city, way above the streets, seeing its lights but cut off from everyone. Neither Ira nor his predecessors can find their places within currents of humanity, for the movements of the works circle a still pool and the direction of the vision is toward stasis. Like her characters, Tyler's readers may also be like Ira's and Maggie's son, "a disbeliever in consequences" (*BL* 221).

Because Tyler does not shy from sentiment but explores the inner emotional depth of her characters, she has been praised by reviewers who object to other contemporary writers' employment of more violent actions and depictions of human beings as cold and unresponsive. The latest books, we saw, were contrasted to current vogues of despair or "worldly cynicism."[13] That she is pessimistic in another way, in presenting the round of human affairs as a perpetual, unchanging cycle beyond the scope of characters' ability to alter has been less forthrightly declared.

Reviewers have long shown dissatisfaction with related aspects of her work, particularly with the "passivity" of her heroes.[14] One reviewer observed in *Breathing Lessons* an incompleteness in the rendering of Ira's sense of wasted life, calling the novel "an oddly skewed work, one which raises expectations it has no intention of meeting."[15] Some have pointed to social issues or class attitudes in her work without judgment, in references to the "postwar conservatism of the 1950s" and the "nostalgia" of Ira's and Maggie's generation.[16] Others have voiced objection to the tone of *Breathing Lessons*, to her "palpable" "distaste" and "condescension" toward the "dreary and dull" lives of the middle-class Morans, and have judged *Breathing Lessons* to be marred by "a dense atmosphere of depressing class signifiers."[17]

One reader raised the question, "Should a reviewer criticize a gifted novelist for seeming to refuse the high moral charge of art?" and answered herself, "No, no, and no!"[18] Other critics who might object seem to have ignored her work, radical feminists or earnest advocates of a new politics of criticism. If such readers —proceeding from a premise that "the motive of feminist criticism cannot be acceptance; it must be resistance in the interest of social transformation through interpretation"[19]—examined Tyler, they might well be blind to her warmth, her charm, her sentiment.

Because Tyler remains a popular writer as well as one treated in the academy, one can wonder, in an old-fashioned way, what plain readers think of her, those not eager to engage in debate over the direction of poststructuralism or hip to the latest in "the phallocentric economy of texts or interpretive strategies."[20]

Large numbers of a composite sort of reader in fact appeared for the

Baltimore symposium on Tyler's work sponsored by Essex Community College in April, 1989, a conference organized before and held just after the announcement of her second major prize in as many works. It was a remarkable gathering from town and gown, a social as well as professional mix of the city so prominent in Tyler's works and participants from many states. Roland Park was there, suburban matrons with careers as civic-minded volunteers, and others with careers in business, in politics, even homemakers of the ilk of many of Tyler's heroines. South Baltimore was there too, at least in the minds of the many teachers in Baltimore who struggle yearly with kids like Muriel's and Maggie's—fatherless second graders who can't subtract, high-school drop-outs, pregnant teenagers. How can we know how the stories Tyler tells comport with their views of the towns they live in—Baltimore, Trenton, Washington, Atlanta, Richmond, Cleveland, Chicago?

If fictions about a town that a writer is busily populating afford even a grain in the balance of readers' judgments of historical process in their lives, these works are weighted toward the view that the solution is in endurance, that toward really changing things there's little to be done. Waste in Tyler's world is of time given to effect change, not waste of life's opportunities for action.

NOTES

1. Peter S. Prescott, Rev. of *Breathing Lessons, Newsweek,* 26 September 1988, p. 73.

2. Joseph Mathewson, "Taking the Anne Tyler Tour" [rev. of *The Accidental Tourist*], *Horizon* 28 (September 1985), 14.

3. Lee Lescaze, "Mid-life Ups and Downs" [rev. of *Breathing Lessons*], *The Wall Street Journal,* 6 September 1988, p. 28.

4. Mathewson, p. 14.

5. Edward Hoagland, "About Maggie, Who Tried Too Hard," *The New York Times Book Review,* 11 September 1988, p. 44.

6. Ibid., p. 1.

7. Jonathan Yardley, "'Tourist,' Lost in the Translation," [rev. of film, *The Accidental Tourist*], *The Washington Post,* 9 January 1989, Sec. B, p. 2.

8. I discuss the question in "Anne Tyler," in *Southern Women Writers, The New Generation,* ed. Tonette Bond Inge (Tuscaloosa: University of Alabama Press, forthcoming 1989).

9. Marguerite Michaels, "Anne Tyler, Writer 8:05 to 3:30," *The New York Times Book Review,* 8 May 1977, p. 13.

10. 1 (1) (April 1989), 28–37.

11. Ibid., pp. 31–35.

12. Ibid., p. 34.

13. Mathewson, p. 14.

14. Mary Ellen Brooks, "Anne Tyler," *Dictionary of Literary Biography,* vol. 6: *American Novelists since World War II, Second Series,* ed. James E. Kibler, Jr. (Detroit: Gale Research, 1980), p. 343.

15. Elizabeth Beverly, "The Tidy Plans that Crumbled" [rev. of *Breathing Lessons*], *Commonweal,* 116 (24 February 1989), 120.

16. R. Z. Sheppard, "In Praise of Lives Without Life-Styles" [rev. of *Breathing Lessons*], *Time,* 5 September 1988, p. 75.

17. David Klinghoffer, "Ordinary People" [rev. of *Breathing Lessons*], *National Review,* 40 (30 December 1988), 49.

18. Beverly, p. 120.

19. Elizabeth A. Meese, *Crossing the Double-Cross: The Practice of Feminist Criticism* (Chapel Hill: University of North Carolina Press, 1986), p. 14.

20. Ibid., p. 137.

Contributors

Doris Betts is Alumni Distinguished Professor of English at the University of North Carolina, Chapel Hill.

Virginia Schaefer Carroll is assistant professor of English at Kent State University, East Liverpool Campus, Ohio.

Barbara Harrell Carson is professor of English at Rollins College, Winter Park, Florida.

Mary J. Elkins is professor of English and department chair at Florida International University, Miami.

Susan Gilbert is professor of English at Meredith College, Raleigh, North Carolina.

Margaret Morganroth Gullette is the author of *Safe at Last in the Middle Years* and many essays about the ideology of aging and contemporary beliefs about the life course.

Sue Lile Inman is instructor of English at Furman University, Greenville, South Carolina.

Theresa Kanoza is instructor of English at Michigan State University, East Lansing.

Carol S. Manning is associate professor of English at Mary Washington College, Fredericksburg, Virginia.

Frank W. Shelton is assistant dean of academic affairs at the University of South Carolina, Salkehatchie.

Gordon O. Taylor is professor of English and chairman of the department at the University of Tulsa.

Joseph B. Wagner is associate professor of English at Kent State University, Stark campus, Canton, Ohio.

Anne Ricketson Zahlan is associate professor of English at Eastern Illinois University, Charleston.

Index